Gerald R. Jensen
Northern Illinois University

Robert R. Johnson, CFA
Association for Investment Management and Research

Jeffrey M. Mercer
Northern Illinois University

The Role of Monetary Policy in Investment Management

The Research Foundation of AIMR™
and Blackwell Series in Finance

Research Foundation Publications

The Role of Monetary Policy in Investment Management

ISBN 0-943205-50-6

Printed in the United States of America

November 2000

3 2280 00759 9277

Editorial Staff
Roger S. Mitchell
Editor

Rebecca L. Bowman
Assistant Editor

Jaynee M. Dudley
Production Manager

Kathryn L. Dagostino
Production Coordinator

Kelly T. Bruton/ Lois A. Carrier
Composition

Mission

The Research Foundation's mission is to identify, fund, and publish research that is relevant to the AIMR Global Body of Knowledge and useful for AIMR member investment practitioners and investors.

Biographies

Gerald R. Jensen is professor of finance at Northern Illinois University, where he teaches in the Review Course for CFA Candidates and the Executive MBA Program. He has published extensively in the leading finance journals, including *Journal of Financial Economics, Journal of Financial and Quantitative Analysis, Journal of Banking and Finance, Financial Analysts Journal*, and *Journal of Portfolio Management*. Professor Jensen was the recipient of research grants from the Investment Analysts Society of Chicago (1997 and 1998) and the Foundation for Managed Derivatives Research (2000). He holds a Ph.D. from the University of Nebraska-Lincoln.

Robert R. Johnson, CFA, is a senior vice president in the curriculum and examinations department at AIMR. Previously, he taught at Creighton University, where he was professor of economics and finance and the recipient of the university's 1994 Robert F. Kennedy Award for Teaching Excellence. Mr. Johnson is the author of more than 40 articles in such publications as *Journal of Financial Economics, Journal of Finance, Financial Analysts Journal*, and *Journal of Portfolio Management*. He holds a Ph.D. from the University of Nebraska-Lincoln.

Jeffrey M. Mercer is associate professor and former chair of the department of finance in the College of Business at Northern Illinois University, where he is the director of the Review Course for CFA Candidates. Prior to rejoining the faculty at NIU, he served as vice president and director of research at Ibbotson Associates of Chicago. Professor Mercer's published work appears in academic and practitioner journals, including *Journal of Financial Economics, Journal of Financial Research, Financial Analysts Journal, Journal of Portfolio Management,* and *Journal of Futures Markets*. He is a member of the Investment Analysts Society of Chicago and AIMR. Professor Mercer holds a Ph.D. in finance from Texas Tech University.

Contents

Foreword

Investors have long regarded monetary policy as a key determinant of investment performance. In the days leading up to a meeting of the Federal Reserve Board of Governors, economists and financial pundits engage in spirited debate about whether or not the Fed will change interest rates, and public comments by Chairman Alan Greenspan and Federal Reserve governors are routinely scrutinized for hints of the direction in which the Fed is leaning. Few experienced investors doubt the importance of Federal Reserve policy to investment performance.

Surprisingly, until the publication of this excellent monograph by Gerald R. Jensen, Robert R. Johnson, CFA, and Jeffrey M. Mercer, little evidence had been provided to document the nature and the strength of the relation between monetary policy and investment performance. Even more surprising is the finding by the authors that shifts in monetary policy, as indicated by directional changes in the discount rate, provide valuable information about asset returns for several months following the discount rate change. This finding is clearly a formidable challenge to the efficient market hypothesis.

Jensen, Johnson, and Mercer begin with a succinct, but not at all superficial, review of monetary policy, including historical and organizational information and a description of the various tools available to the Fed. Next, they make their case that directional changes in the discount rate offer the best signal of shifts in monetary policy, and they support this position both logically and empirically. Many readers will appreciate the fact that although the authors necessarily employ complex statistical procedures in their empirical analyses, they take special care to explain in straightforward terms why they chose a particular statistical approach.

Having established the usefulness of the discount rate to assess monetary policy, they investigate the relation between directional changes in the discount rate and returns on various asset classes. Their results are nothing short of startling: U.S. stock returns are substantially above average for several months following an initial reduction in the discount rate and substantially below average in the wake of an initial increase in the discount rate. Ironically, although bond traders appear to be the group that is most obsessed with monetary policy, the authors find no significant relation between shifts in monetary policy and U.S. bond returns. They find, however, that U.S. short-term fixed-income instruments respond in the opposite direction from stocks to directional changes in the discount rate. They also explore the impact of monetary policy shifts on the performance of various industries and capitalization groupings within the U.S. stock market and on foreign stocks, which further substantiates the importance of monetary policy to investment management.

Jensen, Johnson, and Mercer have produced an invaluable resource not only for those of us who face the challenge of generating superior investment performance but also for anyone with intellectual curiosity about the relation between the economy and the investment markets. The Research Foundation is pleased to present *The Role of Monetary Policy in Investment Management.*

Mark P. Kritzman, CFA
Research Director
The Research Foundation of the
Association for Investment Management and Research

Preface

The Federal Reserve and its role in monetary policy attract a great deal of attention from financial market participants. Fed actions and inactions and market responses to Fed posturing are widely reported by the international media. Global stock and bond markets rise and fall in response to nuances in speeches made by Federal Reserve Board Chairman Alan Greenspan and other Fed officials. In fact, markets often vacillate immediately and dramatically in response to Greenspan's public remarks. Indeed, Greenspan is often cited as being "the second most powerful man on earth" (that is, after the U.S. president), and some have argued that even this assessment underestimates the importance of his position. Financial markets reacted enthusiastically when Greenspan was reappointed to another four-year term as Fed chairman beginning in 2000. The Federal Reserve, or at least Greenspan, now occupies a prominent place in American popular culture, as indicated by a recent television commercial in which an adolescent boy asks, "Do you think the Fed will move on interest rates?"

Fed watching, however, is not a recent phenomenon. Several decades ago, as Louise Yamada describes in her recent book *Market Magic*, the late Edson Gould formulated the "Three Steps and a Stumble" investment rule, which relied on Federal Reserve action, or inaction, on interest rates. In addition, for years, many prominent investment experts have based their investment philosophies, at least partially, on monetary policy. For example, in *Martin Zweig's Winning on Wall Street*, Martin Zweig makes the following observation:

> In the stock market, as with horse racing, money makes the mare go. Monetary conditions exert an enormous influence on stock prices. Indeed the monetary climate—primarily the trend in interest rates and Federal Reserve policy—is the dominant factor in determining the stock market's major direction. (p. 43)

The popular media may take the influence of the Federal Reserve as a given, but for investors, the relationship between Fed monetary policy and security return patterns is a topic that deserves serious examination. This monograph presents substantial evidence that an association exists between monetary conditions and returns to various asset classes. Be advised that we are not suggesting that monetary policy *leads to* these return patterns. We are merely suggesting that economic activity, returns on various asset classes, and monetary conditions are closely related. Our findings indicate that over the past four decades, investors could have used monetary policy to significantly enhance portfolio performance. We believe that these results not only are interesting but that they also have definite investment implications for market participants.

We would like to thank Jack Malvey, CFA, and Colin Fenton for their help in obtaining some of the data employed in this study.

1. Federal Reserve Monetary Policy: A Primer

Does monetary policy exert an important influence on the economy? What are the links between monetary policy and financial markets? How does one gauge the monetary policy stance of the Federal Reserve? What actions does the Federal Open Market Committee (FOMC) take to affect monetary aggregates? Does the Fed rely on more than one "tool" to carry out its objectives? These are but a few of the many important questions we address in this monograph to help the analyst better understand the importance of monetary policy in investment management. This chapter is intended to reintroduce the reader to the Federal Reserve's conduct of monetary policy and to discuss recent developments on the topic.

It is important to note at the outset that the Federal Reserve, as the central bank of the United States, conducts monetary policy to achieve three primary goals: price stability, a high and stable rate of employment, and sustainable and "acceptable" growth in economic output. A fortunate and natural byproduct of the Fed's pursuit of these primary goals is the stabilization of interest rates and foreign exchange rates, which the Fed also wants to attain. Unfortunately, achieving all of these goals can be a difficult balancing act because the actions taken to reach one goal can actually work against the attainment of another goal (e.g., monetary stimulus to promote economic growth can become inflationary). An additional difficulty faced by the Fed is that its actions taken in the conduct of monetary policy can have only two direct consequences—either an increase or a decrease in the banking system's level of "reserves."

The United States operates under a fractional reserve banking system, meaning that depository institutions must maintain idle deposits, called required reserves, at the Fed (a smaller amount is also allowed to be held as vault cash). In general, a bank's level of required reserves is equal to some fraction (called the required reserve ratio) of its deposit liabilities. Banks will often hold balances in excess of the required level, but these balances tend to be minimized because the Fed does not pay interest on them. Total reserves in the system equal required reserves plus excess reserves.

When trying to understand how the Fed works, the easiest approach is to work backward in the chronology of actions taken by the Fed. Ultimately, the

Fed seeks a monetary policy that will achieve its goals for inflation, employment, and economic output. Because the Fed cannot directly change any of these variables, it focuses on *intermediate targets*, such as interest rates or monetary aggregates, that have stable or consistent historical relationships with the objective variables. Similarly, because the Fed cannot directly control the intermediate targets (because its actions can directly influence only the level of reserves), it uses its tools to influence an *operating target*, which can bring about subsequent changes in intermediate targets. Because the operating target needs to be predictably responsive to the Fed's policy tools, the Fed has historically chosen as the operating target either the federal funds rate (the market-determined rate for short-term borrowing and lending of excess reserves) or a measure of bank reserves. Today, the "Fed" funds rate contains much of the information necessary to interpret developments in monetary policy.

In general, the Fed can take an expansionary, neutral, or restrictive monetary policy stance. Furthermore, when following an expansionary or restrictive stance, the Fed applies varying degrees of stringency. The Fed is said to take an *expansionary* monetary policy stance when it acts to increase the level of reserves in the banking system. Its objective in doing so is to achieve a higher growth rate of a monetary aggregate. The Fed would likely support a higher growth rate of money to stimulate economic activity or to sustain a current level of economic activity that it believes is noninflationary (i.e., the move could be taken as a signal that expected inflation is low). Conversely, the Fed is said to take a *restrictive* stance on monetary policy when it acts to decrease the level of reserves in the banking system. In such a case, the Fed's objective is to lower the growth rate of (or actually decrease the level of) a monetary aggregate. The Fed would likely impose a slower growth rate of money to slow economic activity because the current level of economic activity may become inflationary (i.e., the move could be taken as a signal that the future inflation rate is expected to be higher). Finally, the Fed can take a *neutral* stance and attempt to hold the level of reserves relatively constant. The manner in which reserves are related to monetary aggregates is an important component of monetary policy. Before addressing this issue, however, a brief review of the monetary aggregates is useful.

Several monetary aggregates exist, and each provides a unique measure of the *money supply*. The money supply is defined quite loosely, and the term is often used to refer to any one of the monetary aggregates. The primary monetary aggregate is the *monetary base*, which equals currency and coins held by the public plus total bank reserves. Because bank reserves dominate the monetary base, the Fed has the greatest direct control over this aggregate. The remaining aggregates are labeled M1, M2, and M3 and differ by their inclusiveness and level of liquidity. M1 includes currency in circulation and checkable deposits. M2 includes M1 plus savings deposits, time deposits, and money market mutual funds. M3 includes M2 plus several large denomination and longer maturity instruments. The nature of M1 has changed over the past two decades, mostly as a result of the rise in popularity of interest-earning checkable accounts and the innovation of money market deposit accounts. Interest-earning checkable accounts have become a larger portion of M1 and now form a greater savings component in M1 and a lesser medium-of-exchange component. Furthermore, the marketing of money market deposit accounts has increased because banks do not have to hold reserves against these accounts. Partly because of the changing nature of M1, the Fed is now believed to pay relatively more attention to M2 than to M1 when tracking developments in the money supply.

How are banking reserves linked to the monetary aggregates? The answer to this question relies on understanding the *money multiplier* and the *money expansion* process. In their role as lenders, banks play the most important part in the money expansion process. The assets on a typical bank's balance sheet consist mostly of loans, with smaller balances in reserves, vault cash, securities, and property and equipment. If a bank's reserve balances somehow increase so that it holds excess reserves (discussed in detail later in this chapter), it can use these balances to create new loans. As loan customers spend the proceeds of their loan (e.g., pay for a new car), they create new deposits in a second bank (the car dealership deposits the check). This second bank will then hold a fraction of the new deposit as reserves and attempt to lend the remaining amount. This process continues as banks farther down the line lend a portion of the smaller and smaller deposits. The total increase in deposits (or M1 in this simple case) is equal to the increase in reserves multiplied by the money multiplier, which is defined as 1 divided by the reserve requirement ratio. Thus, when reserves increase by $1, the increase in M1 is some multiple of this amount.

If the relationship between banking reserves and monetary aggregates were a constant, the Fed could easily expand M1 by a precise amount. The Fed would simply determine a target growth rate for the monetary aggregate and take actions to increase reserves by the appropriate fraction of the aggregate (given the reserve requirement ratio). Unfortunately, the relationship does not strictly hold when the real-world behavior of banks, borrowers, and lenders is considered. The actions of these participants can lead to money "leakages." Examples of such leakages include increases in the public's desire to hold cash rather than to create new deposits, as well as increases in banks' willingness to hold excess reserves rather than to create new loans. The important point, however, is that the Fed has considerable control over the monetary base and, even with complicating factors, has a relatively good idea of how changes in the base will affect the money supply.

The Fed controls the level of reserves in the banking system with three major tools: (1) reserve requirements, (2) open-market operations, and (3) discount rate policy. Reserve requirement ratios are established by the Fed within limits set by Congress, and these ratios determine the proportion of deposit liabilities that must be reserved. Clearly, the Fed can increase or decrease the level of reserves in the system by increasing or decreasing the reserve requirement ratio. This tool, however, is the least used by the Fed to manipulate the level of reserves because of the large and somewhat unpredictable impact even small changes in the reserve requirement can have on the banking system and the money supply.

The Fed's most commonly used policy tool, open-market operations, involves the open-market purchase or sale of U.S. government securities. Fed policy in this area is conducted by the FOMC, which includes the seven members of the Federal Reserve Board of Governors and the 12 regional bank presidents (only five of whom have a vote at any one time). The committee meets approximately every six weeks, and the Federal Reserve Bank of New York carries out the trading of securities in line with the FOMC's policy directive.

When the FOMC wishes to expand the money supply, it directs the trading desk to buy securities from securities dealers. It pays the dealers for the securities by increasing the reserve balances if the dealer is a bank or by increasing the deposit balance of a nonbank dealer through a reserve deposit. In both instances, the excess reserves of the banking system increase, which the Fed hopes will lead to increased lending by banks and an increase in the money supply through the credit expansion process.

The third monetary policy tool of the Fed involves changing the discount rate. The discount rate is the rate a bank pays for borrowing reserves from the Fed. When the discount rate is high, it is more expensive for banks to meet reserve requirements if they are forced to go to the Fed to cover a temporary shortfall. For this reason, banks are likely not to overextend their reserves by lending to the point of having deficient reserve balances. Thus, higher discount rates are restrictive in nature. When the discount rate is low, banks find it less expensive to borrow from the Fed to meet temporary reserve shortfalls. Thus, banks are more likely to expand their lending at the risk of having deficient reserve balances. For this reason, lower discount rates are expansionary in nature.

4

As a general rule, banks prefer not to borrow often from the Fed because of the increased scrutiny that comes with such borrowing. In contrast, borrowing in the federal funds market is an easy and efficient alternative. Therefore, the extent to which a change in the discount rate affects total banking reserves is difficult to know. Some argue that the discount rate is an important monetary policy tool not so much because of the influence it can have on discount window borrowing but because it is taken as a signal by market participants that the Fed is changing, or confirming a prior change in, its stance on monetary policy. That is, increases in the discount rate might be restrictive not because they affect borrowing but because they signal that the Fed has been, or will be, moving to decrease the level of reserves over time. Others argue, however, that the Fed changes the discount rate simply to keep it aligned with the Fed funds rate. According to this view, if Fed actions result in the Fed funds rate being high relative to the discount rate, an increase in the discount rate can be taken as a confirmation that the Fed is pursuing a tighter policy through higher rates.

The question of whether the Fed affects the real economy through monetary policy has been a point of contention among economists for many years. Keynesian economists believed that the money supply (and thus the manipulation of it through monetary policy) had little relevance in stimulating aggregate economic activity (often referred to by economists as aggregate demand). On the other hand, monetarists believe that monetary stimulus can have substantial effects on both real and nominal economic activity. Today, a growing consensus supports the view that monetary policy has an important short-run influence on the real economy. In the case of expansionary policy, this influence comes through the stimulus of demand by lower real interest rates and an increase in the availability of credit. Many also convincingly argue, however, that monetary stimulus cannot have any real effect in the long run, or even in the short run, if it is anticipated by market participants.

Consistent with the monetarist perspective, the evidence presented in this monograph supports a close association between asset returns and monetary policy. For example, we find that stock returns are higher in periods of expansionary monetary policy than in periods of restrictive policy. We do not provide here a theoretical development of what drives this association. The above discussion, however, does provide some possibilities. First, when the Fed takes an expansionary stance, it acts to lower short-term interest rates. Furthermore, expansionary policy is consistent with the Fed signaling to the market that it expects lower inflation in the future (see Romer and Romer 1996). This signaling leads to lower long-term interest rates. If stock prices equal the sum of all future benefits discounted at an appropriate rate of interest, the overall reduction in interest rates should, all else being equal, cause an increase in stock prices and higher returns. Conversely, when the Fed takes a restrictive stance, it increases short-term interest rates, signaling the market that higher inflation is expected and long-term interest rates will increase. The overall increase in rates leads, all else being equal, to lower stock returns.

Some recent changes in the Fed's willingness to disclose policy developments are noteworthy. Although we do not use the federal funds rate as our primary monetary policy instrument in our empirical analysis, most would agree that this rate, as well as the Fed's target for this rate, conveys a great deal of information about policy. (This view does not set aside the issue of money supply, however, because the Fed ultimately affects the economy through changes in the monetary base.) Beginning in early 1994, the FOMC began disclosing any changes in its target for the federal funds rate (and, of course, any immediate change in the discount rate) at the conclusion of its regular meetings. Additionally, since May 1999, the FOMC has also immediately announced, following its regular meetings, any bias it may have for the future direction of policy (e.g., a bias toward tightening). These two developments have greatly reduced the uncertainty associated with policy developments and are important sources of information for Fed watching. Thus, the information provided by the Fed surrounding its FOMC meetings provides a great deal of information for the analyst in gauging monetary policy. For the period considered in this study, simply knowing this information by itself would have been enough to greatly enhance the performance of an investment manager's portfolio.

2. Measuring Monetary Conditions

In analyzing the association between Federal Reserve monetary policy and capital market returns, an obvious consideration is the procedure used to define the monetary environment. In other words, what technique is appropriate to determine whether the Fed is pursuing an expansive or a restrictive monetary policy at a given point in time? Experts' models often provide different answers and rely on a combination of variables (money supply, interest rates, bank reserves, and open-market operations) to determine the Fed's monetary policy posture. Because of their complexity, these models are operationally impractical investment guides that require constant monitoring of economic and monetary variables, identifying very frequent changes in monetary policy, and relying on subjective classification of the monetary environment (see Jones 1989 for a detailed description of various approaches). Accordingly, for the purposes of this analysis, we define monetary policy periods with reference to one simple and unambiguous parameter: the discount rate.[1]

The Case for the Discount Rate

The discount rate, as described in Chapter 1, is one of the Fed's three principal policy tools (the other two being reserve requirements and open-market operations), but with respect to changing the money supply, the discount rate is commonly considered one of the weaker policy tools. McNess (1993) argues, however, that although the aggregate effect of changes in the discount rate can easily be swamped by a sufficient volume of open-market operations, "the discount rate is not simply an irrelevant ornament in the standard list of the tools of monetary policy" (p. 3). The relevance of the discount rate relates to its value as a signal of monetary policy.

Much evidence indicates that changes in the discount rate are interpreted by the market as signals of the future course of monetary policy. Discount rate increases are frequently seen as signals of tighter money,

---

[1]Note that in Chapter 5, we consider several other methods of classifying the monetary environment and conclude that similar results are obtained from the alternative classification methods and that the discount rate has traditionally been the best of the measures considered for the purpose of providing investment guidance.

higher future inflation, and decreases in the level of economic activity. Discount rate decreases, on the other hand, are viewed as signals of easier future monetary conditions, with lower short-term interest rates and increases in the level of economic activity. Studies by Waud (1970), Pearce and Roley (1985), Smirlock and Yawitz (1985), and Cook and Hahn (1988) focus on the short-term market reaction to discount rate changes and confirm that discount rate increases produce negative announcement-period returns and rate decreases produce positive reactions. The focus of this monograph, however, is the performance of security markets—after a change in monetary policy—over the long run.

If the discount rate is a weak tool for affecting the money supply, why is the discount rate an important indicator of Federal Reserve monetary policy? Discount rate changes are often made at substantial intervals and represent a rather discontinuous tool of monetary policy. The discount rate is an administered rate (as opposed to being market determined) that is moved in discrete steps ranging from 25 to 100 basis points. The Federal Reserve Board of Governors, a public body responsible for determining whether changes in bank money and credit are consistent with the economy's cash needs, establishes the discount rate. Consequently, the discount rate receives considerable attention in the media. The Board of Governors itself has stated that "it is only natural that the business and financial community should commonly interpret a change in the level of Reserve Bank discount rates as an important indication of the trend in Federal Reserve Policy" (Board 1961, p. 46; see also Friedman 1959 for a discussion of this view on the importance of the discount rate).

In this monograph, we classify the monetary environment as either expansive or restrictive according to the most recent discount rate change. The classification of the monetary environment remains the same until the discount rate is changed in the opposite direction because, until such a reversal, the Federal Reserve has not signaled any departure from its previously established policy. Consistent with the traditional view, the period following a decrease in the discount rate is classified as expansive. Further discount rate decreases do not affect the classification of the monetary environment because they only reinforce the policy stance signaled by the initial change. Likewise, a restrictive monetary environment begins when the discount rate is first increased and ends when the discount rate is decreased. For example, in December 1974, the Fed lowered the discount rate from 8 percent to 7.75 percent, signaling the beginning of an expansive monetary policy period. This initial decrease was followed by six more rate decreases over the next three years, the last of which was a decrease to 5.25 percent in

November 1976. In August 1977, the discount rate was increased from 5.25 percent to 5.75 percent, signaling the beginning of a restrictive monetary policy period. This binary classification of the monetary environment is consistent with Jensen and Johnson (1995); Jensen, Mercer, and Johnson (1996); Booth and Booth (1997); and Prather and Bertin (1997).

This study examines monthly return data from July 1960 through December 1998. July 1960 is chosen as the starting point for the sample period for three reasons. First, this date corresponds to the initiation of an expansive monetary period because the discount rate was lowered in June 1960, a move that followed a series of rate increases. Second, beginning in the 1960s, monetary policy has been increasingly used and increasingly recognized as a tool to affect economic conditions. Third, our focus is on security markets in the modern era.

Table 1 provides a listing of the defined monetary environments. In the 38 1/2-year period covered in this study, the Federal Reserve changed the discount rate 90 times—43 increases and 47 decreases, but this period contains only 21 "rate-change series" that, in our view, represent fundamental changes in the monetary environment. (A rate-change series is initiated when the Fed changes the discount rate in the opposite direction of the previous change.) Again, although numerous situations exist in which the Fed has simply adjusted the degree of stringency, our focus is on an unambiguous signal of a broad change in overall Fed policy.

The data in Table 1 support two conclusions about Fed policy and its use of the discount rate. First, the Fed's tendency is to follow a rate change with additional rate changes in the same direction. In the time period examined in this study, the average number of rate changes in a series is 4.3, with 14 as the largest number of changes. In our interpretation, these same-direction rate changes simply confirm the Fed's previously established monetary stance. Second, the Fed seldom reverses direction in the short run. The average monetary environment covers almost two years. The shortest monetary environment is 3 months, and the longest, 44 months. This evidence further supports the contention that the discount rate serves as a signal of the Fed's monetary policy intentions over the coming months.

Consistent with previous research (e.g., see Jensen, Mercer, and Johnson 1996), we do not include the month in which the Federal Reserve changed from an expansive to a restrictive monetary policy or from a restrictive to an expansive policy. These months are omitted for two reasons. First, because our objective is to focus on the long-term relationship between monetary conditions and security returns, we eliminate any announcement-period effect. Second, the return associated with months that mark the

Table 1. Monetary Periods Based on Changes in the Federal Reserve Discount Rate, 1960–1998

Series	Increasing (I) or Decreasing (D)[a]	Month and Year of First Rate Change	Rate Changes in Series[b]	Monthly Observations in Series[c]
1	D	June 1960	2	36
2	I	July 1963	3	44
3	D	April 1967	1	6
4	I	November 1967	3	8
5	D	August 1968	1	3
6	I	December 1968	2	22
7	D	November 1970	5	7
8	I	July 1971	1	3
9	D	November 1971	2	13
10	I	January 1973	8	22
11	D	December 1974	7	31
12	I	August 1977	14	32
13	D	May 1980	3	3
14	I	September 1980	4	13
15	D	November 1981	9	28
16	I	April 1984	1	6
17	D	November 1984	7	33
18	I	September 1987	3	38
19	D	December 1990	7	40
20	I	May 1994	4	19
21	D	January 1996	3	35

[a]Increasing (decreasing) rate series are restrictive (expansive) policy periods.
[b]The study period includes 43 rate increases and 47 rate decreases.
[c]The number of monthly observations in the full sample equals 442, with 235 observations following rate decreases and 207 observations following rate increases. Months that include the first rate change in a series are omitted from the sample.

initiation of a new monetary environment would include both expansive and restrictive days. Accordingly, the sample consists of 442 months—235 months in expansive periods and 207 months in restrictive periods—because measuring returns subsequent to a clearly announced monetary policy change provides results that are more relevant for investors.

Alternative Measures of Monetary Policy

If using a simplistic definition of Fed policy can identify an association between monetary policy and capital market returns, one might conclude that more complex refinements could yield even more significant relationships. Although previous studies have used changes in the discount rate to distinguish between fundamentally different monetary conditions, the procedure is not advocated as the best technique for identifying *minor* changes in the stringency of monetary policy. Accomplishing this task would require a more refined approach that could adjust to more frequent changes (see Thorbecke 1997 and Patelis 1997 for examples). Practical use of such a measure, however, would require more frequent trading, more subjective evaluation, and a highly sophisticated investor.

Although this discussion has demonstrated the *methodological* advantages of using Federal Reserve discount rate changes to differentiate between the two alternative monetary environments, the *effectiveness* of this technique can be judged only by analyzing monetary data for the alternative environments to determine whether the technique is supported by empirical evidence. To assess the validity of our monetary conditions measure, we examine eight alternative measures of monetary activity. **Table 2** reports mean levels and mean percentage changes for the eight different monetary and reserve aggregates for the two monetary environments.

The monetary and reserve measures used for Table 2 are obtained from FRED, a database supported by the Federal Reserve Bank of St. Louis. The descriptor used by the Fed to identify the measures is provided in parentheses to clearly delineate the particular version of the measure used in the analysis. Furthermore, in Table 2 and throughout, in deriving the summary statistics, we omit (for reasons already discussed) the month containing a change in the monetary environment.

The mean levels for the measures clearly demonstrate that monetary and reserve aggregates differ significantly between the expansive and restrictive periods. For all measures, the mean level is significantly higher in expansive monetary periods than in restrictive periods. This observation is consistent with the claim that a decrease in the discount rate signals that the Fed is planning to pursue an "easier" monetary policy in the future. Likewise, the lower levels of monetary and reserve aggregates following rate increases are consistent with the common perception that rate increases are harbingers of "tighter money." The t-statistics confirm that the reported differences are highly statistically significant.

The data for percentage changes provide further evidence for the claim that monetary conditions are markedly different for the two types of monetary periods. The percentage change is examined to investigate the rate of change in the values during the alternative monetary periods. For five of the eight measures, the percentage changes are significantly different in the two peri-

Table 2. Monetary and Reserve Aggregates by Monetary Period, 1960–1998

Measure	Level of Measure (US$ billions)			Percent Change in Level		
	Expansive Period	Restrictive Period	t-Statistic (p-value)	Expansive Period	Restrictive Period	t-Statistic (p-value)
Monetary base (AMBSL)	$ 212.023	$ 152.142	4.56 (0.00)	0.604%	0.517%	2.36 (0.02)
M1 (M1SL)	570.973	441.736	4.02 (0.00)	0.550	0.332	4.74 (0.00)
M2 (M2SL)	2,061.933	1,544.07	4.44 (0.00)	0.652	0.494	5.06 (0.00)
M3 (M3SL)	2,590.122	1,905.569	4.43 (0.00)	0.666	0.614	1.51 (0.00)
Excess reserves (EXCRESNS)	0.708	0.487	6.09 (0.00)	1.912	2.224	−0.16 (0.00)
Nonborrowed reserves (BOGNONBR)	29.224	23.348	4.06 (0.00)	0.525	0.083	2.48 (0.01)
Net free or borrowed reserves (NFORBRES)	0.407	−0.340	11.69 (0.00)	−13.849	3.651	−0.38 (0.71)
Adjusted reserves (ADJRESSL)	38.828	30.390	3.90 (0.00)	0.577	0.273	2.61 (0.01)

Note: Monetary base, M1, M2, M3, nonborrowed reserves, and adjusted reserves are seasonally adjusted. Excess reserves and net free or borrowed reserves are nonseasonally adjusted.

ods. Furthermore, in two of the three cases in which there is not a significant difference in the rate of change, the measure is not seasonally adjusted, which may explain the lack of statistical significance. Seasonal fluctuations may increase the variability in the measures and mask the pattern in the variable.

The findings reported in Table 2 are consistent with previous research. Jensen, Mercer, and Johnson (1996), examining a narrower set of monetary measures, find strong support for the view that changes in the direction of the discount rate serve as effective indicators of broad changes in Fed monetary policy. These results strongly support the contention that a change in the direction of the discount rate is generally associated with subsequent changes in monetary and reserve aggregates in the expected direction. The findings are consistent with the view that the Fed uses changes in the discount rate to signal shifts in monetary policy. This evidence is counter to the findings of Thornton (1998) that discount rate changes are not significantly related to subsequent changes in monetary and reserve aggregates. The contrasting results may be attributable to two main differences in research methodology. First, Thornton treated each discount rate change as a separate event, whereas we argue that the only relevant events are changes in the direction of the discount rate because same-direction rate changes serve only to reinforce the previous rate change. Thus, one would not expect to observe shifts in monetary or reserve aggregates subsequent to such discount rate changes. Second, we examine the monetary and reserve aggregates over the entire monetary period, whereas Thornton focuses on the short-term movement in the aggregates immediately following a discount rate change. In our view, a shift in Fed policy may be reflected in monetary and reserve aggregates gradually and only over an extended period of time.

Summary

The discount rate traditionally has been interpreted as a signal of the Federal Reserve's stance on monetary policy and is used in this study to define monetary periods for several reasons. First, numerous empirical studies document that rate changes provide valuable information to the financial markets. Second, rate changes are shown to delineate periods of substantially differing levels of reserve and monetary aggregates. Third, the discount rate has been advocated by the Fed itself as a tool for gauging policy developments. Finally, the discount rate has been used by the Fed throughout the entire study period. Alternative measures offer few, if any, advantages and are too complicated to be of practical use to investors.

3. Monetary Conditions and the Performance of Stocks and Bonds

Considerable evidence indicates that security returns exhibit predictable patterns. Studies show that changes in monetary and business conditions are significantly related to subsequent security returns. Changes in business conditions—as proxied by variables such as the default premium, the term premium, and the dividend yield—represent the first class of variables shown to predict future stock returns (see Keim and Stambaugh 1986; Campbell 1987; Fama and French 1988, 1989; and Schwert 1990). More recently, studies by Jensen and Johnson (1995); Thorbecke (1997); and Jensen, Johnson, and Mercer (1997, 1998) demonstrate that monetary conditions explain similar patterns in future stock returns. Furthermore, Jensen, Mercer, and Johnson (1996) and Patelis (1997) show that monetary conditions and business conditions are related but not redundant. Specifically, both monetary conditions and business conditions explain significant variation in future security returns, even in the presence of the other measure.

Prominence and Consistency of Return Patterns

This chapter examines several facets related to security returns and monetary conditions to determine the prevalence of the performance patterns in both stock and bond returns. The results should be of particular interest to investors because we measure returns subsequent to a change in the monetary environment. Specifically, we measure returns starting in the calendar month after a change in monetary policy.

To assess the relationship between security returns and monetary conditions, we start by investigating mean monthly returns for eight alternative general indexes, as shown in **Table 3**.[2] The data for the indexes is obtained

---

[2] Note that for the reasons discussed in Chapter 2, we examine security returns for the period starting in July 1960 and continuing through December 1998. Also, as already indicated, months that include a change in the monetary environment are removed from the sample, so the starting date is July rather than June. Months that include the initiation of a new monetary environment are omitted from the return calculation because such months contain days falling in each monetary environment.

Table 3.   Mean Monthly Returns by Monetary Environment, 1960–1998

Index	Entire Sample	Expansive Period	Restrictive Period	t-Statistic (p-value)	Wilcoxon z-Statistic (p-value)
Stock[a]	1.0503%	1.6441%	0.3761%	3.01	–2.71
				(0.00)	(0.01)
30-day T-bill	0.4892	0.4178	0.5703	–7.34	7.36
				(0.00)	(0.00)
90-day T-bill	0.5345	0.4650	0.6134	–6.11	6.74
				(0.00)	(0.00)
1-year T-bond	0.5756	0.5438	0.6117	–1.26	1.11
				(0.21)	(0.27)
5-year T-bond	0.6000	0.6173	0.5802	0.24	–0.73
				(0.81)	(0.47)
10-year T-bond	0.6159	0.6540	0.5726	0.38	–0.42
				(0.70)	(0.67)
30-year T-bond	0.6250	0.7014	0.5382	0.59	–0.50
				(0.56)	(0.62)
CPI	0.3717	0.2712	0.4859	–6.99	6.22
				(0.00)	(0.00)
Sample size	442	235	207		

[a]Stock index is the CRSP value-weighted NYSE, Amex, and Nasdaq index, including dividends.

from the Center for Research in Security Prices (CRSP) index database, and the stock index is the CRSP value-weighted NYSE, Amex, and Nasdaq index, including dividends, which is selected because it best indicates the total return of the general stock market. We also include six U.S. Treasury security indexes that cover the spectrum of maturities. Finally, the percentage change in the consumer price index (CPI) is reported as an indicator of inflation.

The data in Table 3 indicate that for the overall period, the stock market returned an average of 1.05 percent a month (approximately 12.6 percent annually). The shortest-term Treasury securities had a return of 0.49 percent (5.87 percent annually), and the 30-year T-bond returned 0.63 percent (7.5 percent annually). The returns reflect the normal relationships observed between these various asset classes.

The most interesting findings in Table 3 are the prominent return patterns displayed relative to the monetary environment. The evidence indicates that stock returns display an especially strong pattern associated with the monetary environment, with returns more than four times higher in expansive versus restrictive monetary periods. The average stock return on an annualized basis is approximately 19.7 percent during expansive monetary periods and only 4.5 percent during restrictive periods, and a *t*-test clearly demonstrates that this return difference is statistically significant. The substantial difference in returns is especially surprising because we omit the announcement-period returns associated with a change in monetary conditions. The importance of these results for investors is highlighted by the fact that the return patterns *follow* such a widely publicized event (a change in the discount rate). Also, these patterns are consistent with the evidence reported in the previously referenced study (Jensen, Mercer, and Johnson 1996).

To establish the consistency of the return pattern, the Wilcoxon rank-sum test (a nonparametric test) was applied to the monthly returns. As a nonparametric test, the Wilcoxon rank-sum test is less sensitive to outliers in the return series, and it is used to ensure that the return difference is not attributable to a few isolated periods of extreme return performance. The resulting *z*-statistic clearly indicates that the stock return pattern is not caused by a few unusual monthly returns. This observation suggests that the results reflect a systematic relationship between monetary conditions and stock returns. This finding is consistent with the conventional view that an expansive monetary policy is good news for equity investors and a restrictive policy is generally bad news.

Treasury security returns indicate a significant return pattern for the short-term Treasury securities but not for the long-term end of the maturity spectrum. Interestingly, for the short-term Treasuries, returns are superior in *restrictive* periods. Furthermore, the return difference diminishes as the maturity increases—reversing itself for maturities longer than five years. For the 30-day, 90-day, and 1-year Treasuries, the annualized return differences are approximately 183, 178, and 81 basis points, respectively, with the returns during restrictive periods dominating. The Wilcoxon statistics clearly demonstrate that the return patterns for the short-term Treasuries result from a consistent pattern rather than a few isolated return anomalies. For the Treasuries with maturities beyond one year, the returns are higher in expansive periods, but the return differences are statistically insignificant.

Perhaps the most surprising result in Table 3 is that the average stock return during restrictive monetary periods is less than the return for any of the other seven indexes. This result indicates that, on average, a negative relationship existed between risk and return during restrictive periods, because the return to the lower-risk debt instruments exceeded the return on stocks. An inverse relationship between risk and return that persists over such a long period of time is surprising. Furthermore, on average, the *real* stock return (stock return less inflation) was negative during restrictive monetary periods. Once the increase in price level is considered, on average, equity investors actually lost approximately 1.3 percent a year during restrictive monetary periods. This result is caused by a combination of two factors. First, restrictive monetary periods generally exhibited significantly lower stock returns. Second, inflation (as proxied by changes in the CPI) was significantly higher during restrictive monetary periods. In contrast, the *real* annual stock return for expansive monetary periods is approximately 16.5 percent, which indicates that, on average, equity investors were able to achieve dramatic gains in purchasing power during such periods.

Finally, the evidence in Table 3 is consistent with studies finding that changes in business conditions explain significant time-series variation in stock returns (Fama and French 1989; Jagannathan and Wang 1996; and Ferson and Harvey 1999) as well as studies finding evidence of security return patterns that are associated with changes in Fed monetary policy. For example, Fama and French contend that the stock return patterns exist because changes in business conditions cause investors to alter their required returns. The data in Table 3 confirm previous research that finds an association between security return patterns and changes in Fed monetary policy. Both sets of research, the studies relating to monetary policy as well as the studies relating to business conditions, support the view that changes in monetary conditions also influence investors' required returns. (Note that, as already described, although business conditions and monetary conditions are related, studies show that the two measures are not redundant and that each measure relates significantly to stock returns—both separately and in the presence of the other measure.)

The stock return patterns identified in Table 3 become even more surprising when evaluated in light of **Table 4**, which reports standard deviation of returns for the same eight indexes examined in Table 3. Specifically, the standard deviation of the stock index indicates that the stock market has been significantly more (less) volatile during restrictive (expansive) monetary periods. Thus, given the lower risk exhibited by common stock in expansive monetary periods, the performance of the stock market is even more dominant during expansive monetary periods relative to restrictive periods because the stock market produced the superior returns while subjecting investors to significantly less risk. Had the standard deviations been significantly higher during expansive periods, the higher returns could have been explained—at least partially—as representing compensation for a more volatile stock market environment.

Table 4. Standard Deviation of Returns by Monetary Environment, 1960–1998

Index	Entire Sample	Expansive Period	Restrictive Period	F-Statistic (p-value)
Stock[a]	4.4163%	4.0632%	4.7054%	1.34
				(0.03)
30-day T-bill	0.2274	0.1861	0.2427	1.70
				(0.00)
90-day T-bill	0.2615	0.2221	0.2803	1.59
				(0.00)
1-year T-bond	0.5548	0.4701	0.6367	1.83
				(0.00)
5-year T-bond	1.5854	1.4236	1.7544	1.52
				(0.00)
10-year T-bond	2.2143	2.1481	2.2915	1.14
				(0.34)
30-year T-bond	2.9074	2.8344	2.9926	1.11
				(0.42)
CPI	0.3320	0.2503	0.3744	2.24
				(0.00)
Sample size	442	235	207	

[a]Stock index is the CRSP value-weighted NYSE, Amex, and Nasdaq index, including dividends.

The standard deviations for all but the two Treasury securities of longest maturity are also significantly higher during restrictive monetary conditions. This result suggests that restrictive periods were characterized by a higher than average volatility in interest rates. Given the CPI evidence, much of this volatility can probably be attributed to the persistence of a higher rate of inflation during restrictive periods and the occurrence of greater volatility in the inflation rate during such periods. Overall, the data indicate that restrictive monetary periods are generally characterized as being periods of greater financial market volatility.

The evidence reported in Table 3 documents that, on average, stock returns in expansive monetary periods have been significantly higher than the returns earned during restrictive periods. Furthermore, the Wilcoxon statistic indicates that the return difference is not the result of a few extreme observations. This evidence, however, does not indicate whether the relationship between stock returns and monetary conditions has strengthened or weakened over time. For example, the result would be of far less interest to investors if the return differences were prominent in the 1960s and 1970s but were absent or minimal in the 1980s and 1990s. To address this concern, **Table 5** reports inflation-adjusted (real) stock returns for each of the 21 separate monetary environments (as defined in Table 1 of Chapter 1). Real stock returns are reported to allow for a more valid comparison of returns over time because comparing nominal stock returns over time can lead to misleading conclusions. For example, an annual stock return of 12 percent is much more attractive when inflation is less than 2 percent, as was the case during much of the 1960s, whereas the same 12 percent stock return during the early 1980s would have been considered dismal. The Wilcoxon test statistics in Table 3 establish that the stock return patterns are not the result of a few unusual observations. Table 5 confirms this result and indicates that a general reduction or increase in the prominence of the return patterns has not occurred over time. In short, with very few exceptions, stocks consistently performed poorly during restrictive monetary periods but did quite well during expansive periods.

A closer look at the returns produced during the expansive monetary periods provides some interesting observations. Surprisingly, the real

Table 5. Real Stock Returns by Monetary Environment, 1960–1998

Expansive Monetary Periods			Restrictive Monetary Periods		
Number of Months	Mean Real Return[a]	Start of Series[b]	Number of Months	Mean Real Return[a]	Start of Series[b]
36	0.7800%	June 1960	44	0.8157%	July 1963
6	0.3223	April 1967	8	0.5929	November 1967
3	3.3538	August 1968	22	−1.3505	December 1968
7	2.1357	November 1970	3	−0.2698	July 1971
13	1.6615	November 1971	22	−2.8478	January 1973
31	1.2747	December 1974	32	0.1902	August 1977
3	3.7471	May 1980	13	−0.5009	September 1980
28	0.9203	November 1981	6	0.7136	April 1984
33	2.1098	November 1984	38	−0.0762	September 1987
40	0.9454	December 1990	19	1.5189	May 1994
35	1.7725	January 1996			

[a]Mean monthly real returns are reported as percentages. Real stock returns are calculated by subtracting the monthly percentage change in CPI from the monthly return for the CRSP value-weighted NYSE, Amex, and Nasdaq index, including dividends.

[b]As indicated previously, the month containing the first discount rate change of a series is omitted from the sample because the month contains days in both an expansive and a restrictive monetary period.

returns for the 11 expansive monetary periods are all positive. Even the lowest real return, which occurred in 1967, still represented a return of approximately 4 percent on an annualized basis. In addition, several of the returns reported during expansive periods are substantial, and the real return exceeded 2 percent a month in 4 of the 11 expansive environments.

Returns during restrictive monetary periods also provide some interesting observations. The dismal performance of stocks during restrictive monetary periods is highlighted by the observation that real returns were negative in 5 of the 10 restrictive periods. Moreover, only the last restrictive period produced a real monthly return that exceeded 0.9 percent, but during expansive periods, the real returns were higher than 0.9 percent for all but the first two series. This evidence provides strong support for the view that stock returns exhibit a systematic relationship with monetary conditions.

Overall, the real returns indicate that expansive monetary periods consistently provided an attractive investment climate but that restrictive periods were generally poor periods for equity investors. In every expansive monetary period, equity investors made gains in purchasing power, and in 10 of 11 periods, the gains were substantial. In contrast, equity investors lost purchasing power in 5 of 10 periods during restrictive monetary conditions and made substantial gains in only 3 of the 10 periods.

Timing of Return Patterns

Although Tables 3, 4, and 5 provide strong evidence of prominent and consistent security return patterns that are related to monetary policy, one facet of the return patterns has not been considered. Specifically, the performance patterns have not been related to the timing of the change in policy. For example, depending on one's view regarding the delay between the Fed signal of a shift in policy and actual Fed actions, one could argue that the return patterns should be more or less prominent in the first few months after a change in policy.

Table 6 provides empirical evidence for the timing of the return patterns relative to the monetary policy change. The first three columns of Table 6 report mean returns chronologically for the first three calendar months after a change in the monetary environment. The final column reports the average return from month four through the end of the environment. Panel A reports the monthly returns subsequent to the initiation of an expansive monetary period (a period following the first discount rate decrease), and Panel B shows returns subsequent to the initiation of a restrictive period (a period following the first discount rate increase). As previously indicated, the calendar month

Table 6. Returns Following Monetary Environment Changes, 1960–1998

	Monthly Return			
Index	One Month After Rate Change	Two Months After Rate Change	Three Months After Rate Change	Four or More Months After Rate Change
Panel A. Expansive monetary environment				
Stock[a]	3.4207%	3.8260%	1.5573%	1.4332%
30-day T-bill	0.4682	0.4311	0.4487	0.4127
90-day T-bill	0.5742	0.4754	0.4901	0.4571
1-year T-bond	0.6800	0.4840	0.3280	0.5514
5-year T-bond	0.4902	0.1353	−0.2256	0.6964
10-year T-bond	0.2824	0.0113	−0.5929	0.7772
30-year T-bond	−0.1515	−0.1864	−1.1638	0.8977
Panel B. Restrictive monetary environment				
Stock[a]	−2.0533%	−0.6810%	0.3615%	0.5740%
30-day T-bill	0.5010	0.4719	0.5497	0.5809
90-day T-bill	0.5695	0.5171	0.6129	0.6213
1-year T-bond	0.5019	0.4333	0.8762	0.6131
5-year T-bond	0.3215	0.4793	1.5071	0.5482
10-year T-bond	0.2722	0.8887	1.4489	0.5222
30-year T-bond	0.2832	1.1467	1.1946	0.4812

Note: The values reported in the table are mean monthly returns over the relevant calendar month subsequent to the initiation of a new monetary environment and are reported as percentages.

[a]The stock index is the CRSP value-weighted NYSE, Amex, and Nasdaq index, including dividends.

in which a change in the monetary environment occurred is not considered because it includes days in more than one monetary environment.

The data for the stock index demonstrate that the first two months after a change to a new monetary period display the most prominent return patterns. Following the initiation of an expansive monetary period, the mean monthly stock return is approximately 3.4 percent in the first month and 3.8 percent in the second month. In contrast, for the first two months of a restrictive period, on average, the returns are approximately –2.1 percent and –0.7 percent, respectively. For an informationally efficient market in which relevant information is quickly impounded, these observations suggest that unusually positive (negative) news impacts the market after a change to an expansive (restrictive) monetary environment. The mean stock returns from month three and forward are generally consistent within the monetary period, but the level of returns in expansive periods is markedly higher in expansive versus restrictive periods. Specifically, the mean returns from month three and forward are approximately 2.5 times higher in expansive versus restrictive periods.

The long-term (5-, 10-, and 30-year) Treasury indexes display a very unusual pattern following a change in the monetary environment. The return pattern for the first three months is the opposite of the return pattern over the remaining months. Long-term Treasuries perform exceptionally well in the first three months during restrictive periods but perform substantially worse in subsequent months. In contrast, long-term Treasuries perform poorly in the first three months during expansive periods but perform well in subsequent months. Surprisingly, the third month following a change in environment exhibits the most extreme difference in security returns for both expansive and restrictive periods. For the 30-year T-bond, the returns in month three are approximately −1.2 percent and 1.2 percent during expansive and restrictive periods, respectively. Given that the prominent factor influencing shifts in Treasury returns is investor expectations about inflation, it appears that changes in inflation expectations tend to lag monetary policy changes. If the bond markets are relatively efficient with regard to new information (i.e., a rate change), the return behavior observed would be the result of additional information coming to the market after the rate change. In particular, a shift to a restrictive environment would seem to precede "good" inflation news, and a shift to an expansive policy would seem to precede "bad" inflation news.

If no tendency exists for new information to come to the market following rate changes, the above evidence is consistent with the view that bond markets need, on average, about four months after the first rate change to determine the signal in the Fed's action. Romer and Romer (1996) argue that expansionary policy is consistent with the Fed signaling to the market that it expects lower inflation in the future. If this view is true, a rate decrease should lead to lower long-term interest rates. The evidence in Panel A for 10-year and 30-year T-bonds, however, suggests that, on average, it takes four or more months before long-term yields fall and returns increase, as if the bond market initially believes a rate cut contains "bad" inflation news. In a similar manner, Romer and Romer suggest that a change to a restrictive policy signals higher inflation expectations, which should lead to higher long-term yields and lower returns. Panel B, however, shows that returns actually increase monotonically for the first three months after the first rate change before falling to a lower level.

Although short-term Treasuries display a more consistent return performance within monetary environments, a slight trend appears to exist in these returns. For the 30- and 90-day T-bills, the returns tend to diminish slightly over time during expansive periods and tend to increase slightly over time during restrictive periods.

Overall, the evidence indicates that long-term Treasuries experience substantial fluctuations in return patterns not present in short-term Treasuries. This observation suggests that inflation expectations change markedly in the first few months following a change in the monetary environment. The initiation of an expansive (restrictive) monetary period frequently precedes an increase (decrease) in the expected inflation rate.

Finally, **Table 7** shows the statistics on skewness for the various indexes. Note that the equal-weighted index is included in the analysis because small-capitalization stocks generally have more positively skewed returns. The data indicate that stock returns exhibit more favorable skewness during expansive monetary periods. The difference in skewness is especially pronounced for the equal-weighted index because its returns have substantial positive skewness in expansive periods and considerable negative skewness during restrictive periods. This evidence provides even more support for the contention that expansive monetary periods constitute attractive periods for equity investors. The T-bill and short-term Treasuries indexes exhibit more favorably

Table 7. Distribution Characteristics by Monetary Periods, 1960–1998

	Skewness	
Index	Expansive Period	Restrictive Period
Stock, value weighted[a]	–0.1199	–0.6662
Stock, equal weighted[b]	0.6319	–0.7967
30-day T-bill	1.1792	1.3559
90-day T-bill	1.6958	1.9857
1-year T-bond	0.9068	2.6586
5-year T-bond	–0.0034	0.8091
10-year T-bond	0.6403	0.2250
30-year T-bond	0.4908	0.4123
CPI	0.6148	0.6650

Note: Reported returns are calculated from the CRSP index database.

[a]CRSP value-weighted NYSE, Amex, and Nasdaq index.

[b]CRSP equal-weighted NYSE, Amex, and Nasdaq index.

skewed return distributions during restrictive monetary periods, which further supports the claim that short-term Treasuries are attractive investments during such periods. Finally, the longer term Treasuries are more favorably skewed in expansive periods, but the difference is trivial for the 30-year bond.

Summary

Security returns exhibit prominent and consistent return patterns related to changes in the monetary environment. Furthermore, these return patterns follow a change in the discount rate, which is a well-publicized event upon which investors can act. During periods of expansive monetary policy, stocks exhibit higher returns, lower volatility, and a more favorably skewed distribution.

Returns on long-term T-bonds are higher in expansive periods, although the difference is not statistically significant. Interestingly, long-term T-bond returns in the first three months following the initiation of a restrictive environment are substantially higher than returns in the first three months following the initiation of an expansive environment. Finally, T-bills differ from both bonds and stocks in that they have had significantly higher returns in periods of restrictive monetary policy.

4. Monetary Conditions and the Performance of Various Asset Classes

The evidence described in Chapter 3 shows that several general security classes exhibit prominent monetary-policy-related return patterns. Consistent with the importance investment professionals place on asset allocation, this chapter examines the prevalence of similar return patterns for various subcategories of equity securities and investigates whether similar return patterns exist for commodity futures.

One goal of tactical asset allocation (which is of particular interest in the context of this study) is to increase the relative portfolio weights of asset classes that are more likely to benefit from current monetary conditions. The findings reported in Chapter 3 indicate that equity securities as a whole perform poorly during restrictive monetary periods and perform well during expansive periods, but the performance patterns are likely to differ among various types of stocks. To determine the performance of certain equity subcategories relative to monetary conditions, we examine performance in three areas: industry affiliation, international equities, and capitalization. Also, based on empirical evidence suggesting that commodities serve as an inflation hedge, we look at the performance of commodity futures for the two alternative monetary periods.

Industry Affiliation

One prevalent method of allocating assets is based on a stock's industry affiliation. For example, such industries as construction, utilities, and finance are frequently labeled as interest rate sensitive, and accordingly, an asset allocation strategy might adjust the weightings in such industries to correspond with changes in interest rates. Studies by Bernard and Frecka (1983) and Ma and Ellis (1989) examine the performance of various industries relative to changes in the inflation rate and find evidence indicating that industries differ in their potential for hedging against inflation. In related research, Nowak (1993) argues that monetary policy should have a more pronounced influence on interest-rate-sensitive industries and on industries that have a substantial export or import component.

The implication of these studies is that the monetary-policy-related return patterns should differ among industries. To assess this observation, **Table 8** reports performance data for 19 alternative industry indexes and the market index. The industry indexes are defined following the procedure of Moskowitz and Grinblatt (1999) and are listed, along with the Standard Industrial Code (SIC) for each, in Appendix A. The returns for the industries are equally weighted for all companies in the CRSP NYSE, Amex, and Nasdaq return database that are categorized in the appropriate SIC designation. To remain consistent with the derivation of the industry indexes, the market return in Table 8 is represented by the CRSP equal-weighted NYSE, Amex, and Nasdaq index.

For all 19 industries, the mean returns in expansive monetary periods are higher than the returns in restrictive periods. The difference in mean returns is significant at the 5 percent level for all industries, except the mining industry. The largest return differences (return in expansive periods minus return in restrictive periods) occur for the department store, apparel, transportation equipment, and retail industries, with return differences of approximately 31.5 percent, 31 percent, 30.8 percent, and 28.2 percent, respectively, on an annualized basis. The petroleum, mining, railroad, and utility industries report the smallest annualized return differences—approximately 13 percent, 14.1 percent, 15.3 percent, and 16 percent, respectively. Although this evidence suggests that the monetary environment influences all industries similarly, the industries appear to differ substantially in their degree of sensitivity to monetary conditions. The evidence, however, is not consistent with the expectation that interest-rate-sensitive industries should display more prominent return patterns. Rather, the industries with the most prominent patterns appear to be those that rely most heavily on discretionary consumer spending. In contrast, the industries with the smallest return patterns are those that generally represent essential goods for which spending is less a function of discretionary income. This evidence is consistent with the view that changes in monetary conditions coincide with changes in the availability of money for consumer spending. Hence, the industries that are more reliant on discretionary consumer spending appear to be more sensitive to changes in the monetary environment.

The volatility of returns for the various industries follows the same pattern as that identified for the market index (i.e., returns are more volatile during restrictive versus expansive monetary periods). The differences in standard deviation, however, are significant (at the 5 percent level) for only 7 of the 20 indexes.

Table 8. Industry Stock Performance by Monetary Period, 1962–1998 (continued on p. 30)

	Mean Monthly Return			Standard Deviation		
Market/Industry	Expansive Period	Restrictive Period	t-Statistic (p-value)	Expansive Period	Restrictive Period	F-Statistic (p-value)
Market	2.9071%	0.8665%	3.74 (0.00)	5.2342%	5.9190%	1.28 (0.08)
Apparel	3.0983	0.5175	4.18 (0.00)	6.0459	6.5653	1.18 (0.24)
Chemical	2.7989	1.0608	2.93 (0.00)	5.9428	6.1824	1.08 (0.57)
Construction	2.7654	0.5540	3.79 (0.00)	5.6589	6.2621	1.22 (0.14)
Department stores	3.1577	0.5337	4.12 (0.00)	6.4236	6.5940	1.05 (0.71)
Electrical equipment	3.3563	1.1111	3.05 (0.00)	7.1304	7.8863	1.22 (0.15)
Fabricated metals	2.9795	0.9085	3.52 (0.00)	5.6636	6.3368	1.25 (0.11)
Finance	2.8251	0.7276	4.44 (0.00)	4.4463	5.1815	1.36 (0.03)
Food	2.6294	0.7614	4.08 (0.00)	4.2367	5.0759	1.44 (0.01)
Machinery	3.1121	0.9672	3.26 (0.00)	6.4895	6.9494	1.15 (0.32)
Manufacturing	3.2624	1.2582	3.00 (0.00)	6.3478	7.2856	1.32 (0.05)
Mining	2.7740	1.5975	1.76 (0.08)	6.3926	7.2608	1.29 (0.07)
Paper	2.4234	0.7738	3.14 (0.00)	4.8754	5.8207	1.43 (0.01)
Petroleum	2.0797	0.9956	1.98 (0.05)	5.0261	6.1265	1.49 (0.00)
Primary metals	2.2056	0.9841	2.04 (0.04)	5.8461	6.3827	1.19 (0.21)
Railroads	2.5299	1.2531	2.13 (0.03)	5.7717	6.4948	1.27 (0.09)
Retail	3.0864	0.7335	3.92 (0.00)	5.9042	6.3467	1.16 (0.30)
Transportation equipment	3.1713	0.6050	4.20 (0.00)	5.7154	6.7283	1.39 (0.02)

Table 8. Industry Stock Performance by Monetary Period, 1962–1998 (continued)

Market/Industry	Mean Monthly Return			Standard Deviation		
	Expansive Period	Restrictive Period	t-Statistic (p-value)	Expansive Period	Restrictive Period	F-Statistic (p-value)
Transportation (other)	2.7737%	0.9415%	2.99 (0.00)	5.4978%	6.9304%	1.59 (0.00)
Utilities	1.9318	0.5971	3.86 (0.00)	3.4423	3.6183	1.10 (0.47)

Note: Sample period includes 211 months in expansive monetary environments and 207 months during restrictive periods.

According to the evidence in Table 8, traditional "defensive" industries are generally more favorable investment vehicles during restrictive monetary periods and "cyclical" industries generally make more attractive investments during expansive periods. Rather than focusing on identifying the industries to emphasize during a particular monetary environment, perhaps the most useful approach for investors is to focus on deemphasizing certain industries. For example, because the apparel, construction, and department store industries have annualized returns of less than 7 percent in restrictive monetary periods, investors should avoid these industries during restrictive periods. On the other hand, during expansive periods, investors should underweight the utility, petroleum, and primary metal industries, which substantially underperform the average industry.

International Equities

In recent years, international equities have received increased attention as an investment vehicle for U.S.-based investors. International equities offer two potential advantages for a U.S. equity investor. First, international equities have the potential to provide a higher rate of return than U.S. stocks. Second, international securities may offer diversification benefits if the correlation with U.S. stocks is materially less than perfect. Indeed, much of the original interest for investing in international securities stemmed from the substantial diversification benefits indicated by Grubel (1968), Levy and Sarnat (1970), Solnik (1974), and Lessard (1976).

Even though some researchers question the benefits associated with investing in international equities (e.g., Sinquefield 1996), Gorman (1998) contends that international securities continue to be an attractive investment. Gorman claims that one factor that has kept down the correlations of international equities is the nonsynchronized monetary policies pursued by the various countries. In other research, however, Conover, Jensen, and Johnson (1999a, 1999b) support the relevance of monetary policy in the international investment decision and present evidence of a strong relationship between U.S. monetary policy and the returns on international equities.

To examine such a potential relationship with U.S. monetary policy, the data in **Table 9** show the performance of international stocks for the two alternative U.S. monetary environments. Because of the limited availability of the international indexes, the sample period begins in 1970 and ends in 1998. The U.S. stock index is reported for the same time period to make the results comparable.

The stock return pattern shown previously to be related to U.S. monetary periods prevails in both the U.S. and international markets, as shown in Table 9. This observation further supports the contention that the return pattern represents a systematic relationship and is not merely coincidental. Surprisingly, on average, the return pattern is actually more prominent in the international markets than in the U.S. market. On an annualized basis, during expansive monetary periods, returns are approximately 23 percent and 21.5 percent for the Europe/Australasia/Far East (EAFE) Index and the U.S. market, respectively. The corresponding returns during restrictive periods are approximately 0.1 percent and 3 percent. The prevalent return pattern in

Table 9. Global Market Performance by Monetary Period, 1970–1998

	Mean Monthly Return			Standard Deviation		
Index	Expansive Period	Restrictive Period	t-Statistic (p-value)	Expansive Period	Restrictive Period	F-Statistic (p-value)
EAFE[a]	1.9133%	0.0073%	3.53 (0.00)	4.6602%	5.1267%	1.21 (0.22)
World[b]	1.7929	0.0813	3.66 (0.00)	3.7783	4.5316	1.44 (0.02)
U.S. stock[c]	1.7896	0.2601	2.91 (0.00)	4.0373	5.2113	1.67 (0.00)

Note: The sample period coincides with the availability of the (Morgan Stanley Capital International) MSCI stock indexes. The period includes 190 months in expansive monetary periods and 143 in restrictive periods. As previously indicated, months that include a change in monetary environment are excluded from the sample.

[a]Europe, Australasia, and Far East Index.
[b]MSCI World Index.
[c]CRSP value-weighted NYSE, Amex, and Nasdaq index, including dividends.

international equity markets suggests that the U.S. monetary environment plays a prominent role in both U.S. and international financial markets. In addition, this finding indicates that during restrictive U.S. monetary periods, a strategy of allocating assets away from the U.S. equity market and into international equities would have been detrimental to portfolio performance.

Finally, consistent with U.S. equities, the EAFE Index also exhibits a higher standard deviation of returns in restrictive versus expansive monetary periods. The difference in standard deviations between the two periods, however, is not statistically significant.

The results in Table 9 are consistent with previous evidence. Conover, Jensen, and Johnson (1999a, 1999b) examine stock returns for 15 non-U.S. countries and find that these stock markets exhibit a consistent pattern in relation to the U.S. monetary environment. The strategy of allocating assets away from the U.S. market during restrictive monetary periods in order to avoid the poor performance of the U.S. market appears to be of limited benefit, but on average, non-U.S. markets seem to make more attractive investments during *expansive* U.S. monetary periods.

To select an investment vehicle that helps to diversify away the adverse returns associated with a restrictive U.S. monetary period, one must identify an asset class that displays returns that do not mimic the return patterns of U.S. equities. Although the returns of the EAFE Index suggest that international securities are unlikely to offer much benefit in hedging against adverse U.S. monetary conditions, the emerging markets hold more promise. The strong relationship between EAFE Index returns and U.S. monetary conditions may result from the tendency of monetary authorities in developed countries to cooperate when setting monetary policy, but the degree of cooperation between the monetary authorities in *emerging market* countries and the Federal Reserve, however, is likely to be less pronounced.

If emerging market monetary authorities set policy that is less synchronized (relative to developed market monetary authorities) with Fed policy, then emerging markets may provide a more attractive diversification vehicle relative to developed markets. For an informal test of this proposition, we constructed a value-weighted index of 15 emerging stock markets and examined the returns during the two alternative monetary environments. The returns for the emerging market index are not reported in Table 9 for two reasons. First, the returns are available only from 1976 to the present, so the time availability is somewhat limited. Second, unlike the other market indexes used in the study, the emerging market index is not a widely reported market index but rather an index constructed from individual country indexes. The mean annual returns (calculated in U.S. dollars) for the emerging market index during expansive and restrictive periods are approximately 21.6 percent and 12.8 percent, respectively. The emerging markets display the same general return pattern as U.S. and EAFE markets—with higher (lower) returns in expansive (restrictive) monetary periods—but the returns during restrictive periods are substantially higher than restrictive-period returns for the U.S. and EAFE markets. Because of the problems with return data for emerging markets, this evidence is less robust than evidence for EAFE markets and the U.S. market, but the data suggest that emerging markets may offer an opportunity to hedge against adverse U.S. monetary policy.

Capitalization

Numerous studies present evidence identifying a premium associated with investing in small-cap stocks (see Banz 1981; Basu 1983; Rosenberg, Reid, and Lanstein 1985; Reinganum 1988; Jacobs and Levy 1989; Keim 1990; Harris and Marston 1994; Fama and French 1995; and Cole, Helwege, and Laster 1996). The findings from these studies indicate that even after the higher risk associated with investing in small-cap stocks is controlled for, small-cap stocks produce excess returns.

A few studies have extended the market capitalization research by considering the influence that monetary conditions have on the small-cap premium. Gertler and Gilchrist (1994) argue that the premium may vary with monetary conditions. Specifically, they claim that small-cap stocks are more heavily bound by credit constraints, and thus, monetary policy should have a greater effect on small-cap stocks relative to large-cap stocks. Jensen, Johnson, and Mercer (1997, 1998) present evidence suggesting that the small-cap premium is more prominent during expansive monetary periods.

Table 10 reports evidence on the influence that market capitalization has on the monetary-policy-related stock return patterns. Mean monthly returns and the standard deviation of returns are reported for 10 size deciles for the two monetary environments. The evidence indicates that the return pattern prevails for all levels of market capitalization. The return differences for all 10 deciles are highly significant, both economically and statistically. The largest difference in returns belongs to the smallest-cap decile, with the annual return being approximately 22.2 percent higher in expansive versus restrictive monetary periods. The largest-cap stocks experienced the smallest annual return difference of approximately 14.6 percent. At face value, the return differences suggest that the pattern is stronger than average for small-cap stocks and weaker than average for large-cap stocks, but the t-statistics indicate the opposite: The t-statistic is 2.58 for the smallest-cap stocks and 3.00 for the largest. The much lower (higher) return variation exhibited by

Table 10. Stock Performance for Size Deciles by Monetary Period, 1960–1998

	Mean Monthly Return			Standard Deviation		
Decile	Expansive Period	Restrictive Period	*t*-Statistic (*p*-value)	Expansive Period	Restrictive Period	*F*-Statistic (*p*-value)
Small	2.610%	0.757%	2.58 (0.01)	7.677%	7.361%	1.09 (0.54)
2	2.203	0.432	2.77 (0.01)	6.436	7.017	1.19 (0.20)
3	2.025	0.371	2.71 (0.01)	6.066	6.784	1.25 (0.10)
4	2.004	0.350	2.81 (0.01)	5.862	6.515	1.24 (0.12)
5	1.964	0.267	2.94 (0.00)	5.563	6.467	1.35 (0.03)
6	1.904	0.304	2.85 (0.00)	5.425	6.257	1.33 (0.03)
7	1.824	0.359	2.70 (0.01)	5.157	6.119	1.41 (0.01)
8	1.863	0.377	2.90 (0.00)	4.921	5.758	1.37 (0.02)
9	1.781	0.382	2.91 (0.00)	4.593	5.399	1.38 (0.02)
Large	1.585	0.371	3.00 (0.00)	4.000	4.520	1.28 (0.07)

Note: Performance statistics are calculated from the returns reported for the market-capitalization-based deciles on the CRSP index tape.

stocks with large (small) capitalizations explains the contradiction between the return difference and its level of significance.

The absolute size of the small-cap premium (small-decile return minus large-decile return) is substantially larger during expansive versus restrictive monetary periods. On an annualized basis, during expansive monetary periods, the return for small-cap stocks exceeded the return for large-cap stocks by more than 12 percent. In comparison, during restrictive periods, the small-cap premium was less than 5 percent. These findings indicate that investing in small firms was a more favorable strategy during expansive monetary periods, and furthermore, the results are consistent with the evidence previously reported by Jensen, Johnson, and Mercer (1997, 1998).

For each of the 10 deciles, the difference in risk for expansive versus restrictive monetary periods is not nearly as striking as the return differences. Specifically, the differences of standard deviation are statistically significant (at the 5 percent level) in only five of the deciles, although the differences are nearly significant in several additional deciles. Surprisingly, for the smallest-cap decile, the standard deviation is actually higher during expansive periods. The other nine deciles exhibit a higher standard deviation during restrictive monetary conditions, and the risk difference is generally more prominent for the larger-cap stocks.

The evidence in Table 10 supports the prominence of the monetary-environment-related stock performance pattern. In general, stocks of all capitalizations perform poorly during restrictive monetary periods and perform well during expansive monetary periods. For the entire capitalization spectrum, stock returns are approximately 3.5–5 times higher during expansive versus restrictive monetary periods. In addition, the standard deviation of returns is approximately 10–20 percent higher during restrictive periods. This evidence provides additional support for the contention that a systematic relationship exists between stock performance and monetary conditions.

Commodity Futures

Commodity futures are increasingly being considered for inclusion in investors' portfolios (e.g., see Jensen, Johnson, and Mercer 2000). The attraction of commodity futures is based on two characteristics. First, several authors claim that commodity prices tend to have low correlations with security returns (see Bodie and Rosansky 1980; Irwin and Brorsen 1985; Lee, Leuthold, and Cordier 1985; Irwin and Landa 1987; Elton, Gruber, and Rentzler 1987; and Edwards and Park 1996). Chance (1994) notes, however, that this low correlation is marked by considerable instability. In particular, futures have exhibited both positive and negative correlation with stocks and bonds over time. This observation raises questions regarding the use of futures as a consistent diversification vehicle.

A second and common justification for including commodity futures in a portfolio is the view that they provide an inflation hedge (see Bodie 1983; Irwin and Landa 1987; Edwards and Park 1996; and Bjornson and Carter 1997). As commodity prices increase during an inflationary period, long positions in commodity futures benefit while security returns tend to be adversely affected. Thus, commodity futures may provide investors with a hedge against an adverse inflationary environment.

Consider the performance of the Goldman Sachs Commodity Index (GSCI) for the two alternative monetary periods. **Table 11** reports the

Table 11. Commodity Futures Performance by Monetary Periods, 1970–98

	Mean Monthly Return			Standard Deviation		
Index	Expansive Period	Restrictive Period	t-Statistic (p-value)	Expansive Period	Restrictive Period	F-Statistic (p-value)
GSCI	0.3181%	1.9465%	−2.76 (0.00)	4.4012%	5.9368%	1.82 (0.00)
Stock[a]	1.7896	0.2601	2.91 (0.00)	4.0373	5.2133	1.67 (0.00)

Note: The sample period coincides with the availability of the GSCI. The period includes 190 months in expansive monetary periods and 143 in restrictive periods. As previously indicated, months that include a change in monetary environment are excluded from the sample.

[a]CRSP value-weighted NYSE, Amex, and Nasdaq index, including dividends.

performance statistics for commodity futures relative to monetary conditions. In this analysis, we use the GSCI total return index, which represents the return from a fully collateralized commodity futures investment and is designed to be comparable to an investment in stocks or bonds. The total return equals the return for the futures contract plus the T-bill rate earned on the face value of the futures. (Appendix B describes the composition and construction of the GSCI.) Once again, the stock index is the CRSP value-weighted NYSE, Amex, and Nasdaq index, which is presented for comparison purposes.

The return pattern exhibited by the GSCI in relation to the monetary environment has a magnitude that is comparable with the return pattern for stocks. The GSCI return pattern, however, is the inverse of the stock return pattern. Specifically, on an annualized basis, the GSCI return is approximately 3.8 percent during expansive periods and 23.4 percent during restrictive periods, but over the same monetary periods, the stock returns were approximately 21.5 percent and 3.1 percent.

The GSCI return patterns further support the contention that the security return patterns that we linked to monetary conditions may be at least partially attributed to inflationary considerations. The GSCI is a proxy for the return from taking long positions in commodity futures contracts. An unexpected increase in commodity prices is generally synonymous with an increase in inflation, which, because of the long position in commodity futures, results in a positive return to the GSCI. Thus, a shift to a restrictive monetary policy appears to precede a heightened inflationary environment, and a shift to an expansive monetary policy appears to precede a period characterized by lower inflation concerns. (Note that Table 3 in Chapter 3 shows that, in fact, the rate of inflation is significantly higher during restrictive relative to expansive monetary periods.)

Although most securities demonstrate significantly better performance during expansive monetary periods, this research shows that two asset classes—T-bills and commodity futures—demonstrate significantly better performance during restrictive monetary periods. The difference in return patterns between these two assets and the various equity securities may be explained by the observation that changes in inflation expectations affect these two assets differently than most assets. As a short-term security, T-bills are subject to little interest rate risk and thus can serve as an inflation hedge (see Ankrim and Hensel 1993 and Fama and Schwert 1977). Overall, the return patterns displayed by T-bills and commodity futures support the view that these two securities serve as effective hedges against the adverse returns most securities experience during restrictive monetary environments.

The GSCI standard deviations support the claim that restrictive monetary periods are characterized by relatively high risk. This finding is consistent with the volatility evidence for equities and fixed-income securities. The combination of both types of evidence indicates that restrictive monetary periods entail significantly more risk for financial market participants than do expansive monetary periods.

Summary

Evidence presented in this chapter suggests that traditional "defensive" industries (e.g., chemical, petroleum, mining, and railroad) generally have better performance than other industries during restrictive monetary periods, whereas traditional "cyclical" industries (e.g., apparel, department store, and retail) generally have better performance than other industries during expansive monetary periods. Although all industries have higher returns during expansive policy periods, perhaps the most useful approach for investors is to deemphasize certain industries during expansive periods (e.g., utilities, petroleum, and primary metals) and others during restrictive periods (e.g., apparel, construction, and department store).

Regarding international equities, developed country markets (as proxied by the EAFE index) display return patterns similar to U.S. equity markets. These markets thus offer little potential to hedge against adverse U.S. monetary conditions. The results further provide limited evidence that emerging markets offer some diversification potential; on average, emerging markets perform much better than developed markets during periods of restrictive U.S. monetary policy.

The evidence shows that stock returns in all market-capitalization deciles are significantly higher in expansive policy periods, especially for small-cap stocks. Furthermore, the small-cap premium is quite large during expansive policy periods and (except for the smallest-cap decile) virtually nonexistent during restrictive periods.

Commodity futures are often advocated as a means to hedge against the negative effects of inflation. Examining the GSCI, we find that its return difference in expansive-versus-restrictive policy periods is similar in magnitude to the U.S. stock return difference. Importantly, however, as with the T-bill return differences presented earlier, the GSCI returns are higher in restrictive policy periods. Thus, like T-bills, commodity futures provide equity investors with an effective hedge against restrictive monetary policy (and the higher inflation associated with it).

5. Assessing the Performance of Alternative Monetary Policy Measures as Predictors of Stock Returns

Throughout the analysis presented thus far in this monograph, changes in the Federal Reserve discount rate have served as a broad measure to distinguish between expansive and restrictive periods of monetary policy. Furthermore, evidence presented in Chapter 2 supports the argument that changes in the discount rate are a signal of future monetary conditions. It would be naive, however, to conclude that the discount rate is the only viable policy measure that an investment manager can use to improve investment performance through Fed monitoring. This chapter presents a brief review of the literature that supports the use of alternative monetary policy measures to gauge the Fed's policy stance. We also present empirical evidence showing how well (or poorly) these alternative measures compare with each other and with changes in the discount rate in explaining stock returns.

Research on Alternative Measures

A widely cited study by Bernanke and Blinder (1992) attempts to isolate a direct measure of Federal Reserve policy and link it to measures of economic activity. Bernanke and Blinder present persuasive arguments and empirical evidence that the federal funds rate and the spreads between the federal funds rate and alternative market rates are excellent indicators of Federal Reserve policy. The authors find that the spread between six-month commercial paper rates and six-month T-bill rates tends to dominate other market rates in predicting economic activity (i.e., it has a higher significance level than other measures in a Granger-causality setting). Variance decompositions, however, show that the federal funds rate explains more of the variability in economic activity than do other measures. Stock and Watson (1989), Bernanke (1990), and Friedman and Kuttner (1992) also support the importance of the commercial paper–T-bill spread.

Laurent (1988) and Bernanke and Blinder (1992) show that the spread between the funds rate and a long-term Treasury rate and the spread between the funds rate and a short-term T-bill rate are useful monetary indicators. In a theoretical model of the federal funds market, Ho and Saunders (1985) show that the spreads between the funds rate and other short-term money market rates are linked to the Fed's underlying strategy for monetary policy. Relying on the evidence of previous research, Ogden (1987, 1990) uses the funds rate–T-bill spread as a measure of monetary stringency in an investigation of the link between stock returns and aggregate liquidity. Bernanke (1990) includes the spread between the funds rate and the 10-year Treasury rate in his study and finds it to be a useful indicator of monetary policy.

The spread between short-term and long-term Treasury securities (or "term spread") serves as an indicator of inflation expectations and has been advocated by many researchers as a measure of business conditions (e.g., see Fama and French 1989; Fama 1990; and Schwert 1990). Furthermore, Jensen, Mercer, and Johnson (1996) show that this measure is closely related to monetary conditions.

Empirical Analysis

To determine whether these alternative indicators are associated with stock returns, we examine simple and multiple regressions of stock returns against each of the following six measures:

- Changes in the federal funds rate (ΔFF).
- The difference between the 10-year T-bond rate and the 1-year T-note rate (TERM).
- The difference between the federal funds rate and the 10-year T-bond rate (FF10).
- The difference between the federal funds rate and the three-month T-bill rate (FFTB).
- The difference between the six-month commercial paper rate and the six-month T-bill rate (CPTB).
- A dummy variable equaling 1 in all months following discount rate increases and zero in all months following discount rate decreases (ΔDIR).

All interest rates are monthly averages of daily figures and are lagged one month relative to the returns they are "predicting" in the regressions. The simple regression results are shown in **Table 12**.

The *t*-statistics in Table 12 demonstrate that all of the indicators, except the spread between the commercial paper rate and the T-bill rate, are significant in explaining monthly returns. The dummy variable for the change in the discount rate and the measure for changes in the federal funds rate have a higher adjusted R^2 than the other variables, which indicates that these two measures explain a higher level of the variation in stock returns relative to the

Table 12. Simple Regressions of Stock Returns on Alternative Monetary Policy Measures, 1960–1998

Regression	ΔFF	TERM	FF10	FFTB	CPTB	ΔDIR	Adjusted R^2
			Regression Coefficients and t-Statistics[a]				
1	−0.78						0.0132
	(−2.63)						
2		0.39					0.0065
		(1.97)					
3			−0.28				0.0108
			(−2.41)				
4				−0.52			0.0070
				(−2.02)			
5					−0.58		0.0012
					(−1.24)		
6						−1.27	0.0183
						(−3.04)	

Note: Estimated regressions include an intercept term and the monthly stock return for the CRSP value-weighted NYSE, Amex, and Nasdaq index as the dependent variable.

[a]t-Statistics are in parentheses.

alternative measures. Note that a low R^2 is characteristic of regression models that are developed to explain future monthly stock returns because the stock market is known to behave largely as a random walk. A substantially higher R^2 is achieved with regressions that explain quarterly and semiannual returns. These higher R^2 results occur because of the reduction in "noise" that occurs when long-term returns are used as the explanatory variable.

The findings reported in Table 12 show that the TERM spread is the only variable that is positively associated with stock returns. This observation supports the view that stock returns tend to increase when the yield curve steepens (this contention is also reflected by the negative coefficient on FF10, which also measures the slope of the yield curve but with the opposite sign). A steepening yield curve often reflects increasing levels of economic activity, which is frequently preceded by a strong stock market. Alternatively, a steepening yield curve could also reflect an expansive Fed policy with cuts in short-term rates, which are associated with strong markets.

ΔFF and ΔDIR are negatively related to stock returns because, as described in Chapter 2, stock returns tend to be lower when the Fed is following a restrictive policy and raising short-term rates, whereas returns are higher when the Fed is pursuing an expansive policy and lowering rates. The negative relationship between FFTB and stock returns shows that when the

Fed increases (decreases) the federal funds rate relative to the T-bill rate, it is moving in a more restrictive (expansive) direction and stock market returns weaken (strengthen).

Table 13 provides evidence on whether any or all of the alternative indicators provide information for stock returns that is not provided by the discount rate dummy variable. As shown in the first five regressions, only changes in the federal funds rate add significantly to the discount rate in forecasting stock returns. Interestingly, of ΔFF and ΔDIR, ΔDIR has the stronger forecasting ability, even though it is by far the less sophisticated measure. The superior forecasting ability displayed by ΔDIR is surprising because ΔFF changes on a monthly basis, whereas ΔDIR is a dummy variable that changes infrequently. For the sixth regression, all of the alternative indicators are included, ΔDIR is excluded, and ΔFF is the only significant contributor. When ΔDIR is added back in for the seventh regression, the adjusted R^2 is decreased from the first regression, which included ΔFF and ΔDIR. This observation reflects the irrelevant noise added by the other four alternative indicators.

Table 13. Multiple Regressions of Stock Returns on Alternative Monetary Policy Measures, 1960–1998

| Regression | Regression Coefficients and t-Statistics[a] | | | | | | Adjusted R^2 |
	ΔFF	TERM	FF10	FFTB	CPTB	ΔDIR	
1	−0.61					−1.08	0.0252
	(−2.02)					(−2.53)	
2		0.06				−1.20	0.0162
		(0.23)				(−2.31)	
3			−0.13			−1.02	0.0181
			(−0.95)			(−2.07)	
4				−0.31		−1.11	0.0191
				(−1.17)		(−2.54)	
5					−0.11	−1.24	0.0162
					(−0.21)	(−2.78)	
6	−5.00	−0.37	−0.49	−0.09	−0.43		0.0143
	(−2.12)	(−0.59)	(−0.98)	(−0.15)	(0.52)		
7	−4.34	−0.68	−0.51	−0.13	0.57	−1.12	0.0224
	(−1.84)	(−1.06)	(−1.02)	(−0.21)	(0.70)	(−2.14)	

Note: Estimated regressions include an intercept term and the monthly stock return for the CRSP value-weighted NYSE, Amex, and Nasdaq index as the dependent variable.

[a]t-Statistics are in parentheses.

Finally, **Table 14** presents the correlation coefficients between all pairs of the policy indicators. Consistent with the regression evidence shown for Table 13, the data show a significant level of redundant information contained in TERM, FF10, FFTB, and CPTB (e.g., a –0.91 correlation coefficient between TERM and FF10 and a 0.80 correlation coefficient between FFTB and CPTB). Interestingly, although ΔDIR is significantly correlated with all of the other variables, it is least correlated with ΔFF. In turn, ΔFF is generally not highly correlated with the other four alternative policy indicators. The relatively high correlation between TERM and the other monetary indicators suggests that in studies that have used TERM as a measure of business conditions, the measure was probably serving as an indicator of monetary conditions.

Summary

The evidence indicates that the federal funds rate provides significant information for the future direction of the stock market. Furthermore, because of the imperfect covariation between changes in the federal funds rate and changes in the discount rate, the two policy measures provide complementary information. This finding is consistent with the notion that the discount rate is viewed as a broad measure of the Fed's policy stance. Because the Fed does not often change the discount rate, it provides a signal of the intermediate- to long-term direction of monetary policy, whether tightening or easing. On the other hand, the federal funds rate, being the operating target that the Fed manipulates directly and frequently, is a more refined measure of policy and provides more-detailed information about short-term policy moves. The implication of this finding is that investment managers should be aware of both the Fed's fundamental policy stance and the degree of stringency or leniency the Fed is applying.

Table 14. Summary Statistics and Correlations for Alternative Monetary Policy Measures, 1960–1998

Measure	Mean	Standard Deviation	ΔFF	TERM	FFTB	FF10	CPTB
ΔFF	0.441%	9.18%	1				
TERM	0.744	1.07	–0.18*	1			
FFTB	0.621	0.82	0.07	–0.52*	1		
FF10	–0.759	1.77	0.14*	–0.91*	0.77*	1	
CPTB	0.535	0.45	–0.02	–0.54*	0.80*	0.70*	1
ΔDIR	0.468	0.50	0.17*	–0.62*	0.36*	0.80*	0.41*

*Significant at the 1 percent level.

6. Investment Implications and Conclusions

Investment professionals are well aware of the prominent role that the Federal Reserve plays in the financial markets, yet the empirical relationship between Fed policy and security returns has not been rigorously evaluated. Attempting to fill the void, this monograph examines the relationship between Federal Reserve monetary policy and the returns of a diverse set of securities. Our empirical analysis demonstrates that systematic patterns exist between monetary conditions and security returns. Furthermore, the patterns are shown to be both economically and statistically significant. This chapter highlights the results that have the most practical significance for investment professionals.

General Findings

In general, restrictive monetary conditions tend to depress the performance of most securities, whereas the majority of securities prosper during an expansive monetary policy. Common stocks exhibit the most extreme return patterns. Stock returns during expansive monetary periods are approximately four to five times higher than returns during restrictive monetary periods. Stock returns also exhibit less volatility during expansive versus restrictive monetary periods.

When the sample is differentiated by expansive and restrictive periods of U.S. monetary policy, international equities exhibit return performance patterns comparable to U.S. stock return patterns. Although U.S. investors may be tempted to increase their international equity exposure during a period of restrictive Fed monetary policy, our findings show that such a strategy, if carried out with Europe/Australasia/Far East (EAFE) stocks, would actually be detrimental to portfolio performance. Emerging market stocks, however, may offer a benefit for U.S. investors who overweight these stocks during periods of restrictive U.S. monetary policy. Unfortunately, the robustness of these findings is limited because return data for emerging markets is available only for a relatively short time frame.

The long-term fixed-income market also provides little diversification relief from a restrictive monetary policy because returns for long-term Treasuries are higher (lower) during expansive (restrictive) monetary periods.

This evidence suggests that tactical allocation strategies designed to shift assets from common stocks to long-term bonds when the Fed initiates a restrictive policy would reduce portfolio returns.

Equity subcategories formed on the basis of industry affiliation and market capitalization show the same superior performance during expansive monetary periods. Because the prominence of the return patterns varies by industry and level of capitalization, tactical asset allocation models should incorporate monetary policy when making investment decisions that target these subcategories. The findings imply that the greatest benefit is achieved by using monetary conditions to identify industries that should be avoided at a particular time. Specifically, investors would have been better off under-weighting stocks from the apparel, construction, and department store industries during restrictive monetary periods and underweighting utility, petroleum, and primary metal stocks during expansive monetary periods.

The most promising results for investment applications are observed for T-bills and commodity futures. These are the only two asset classes found to exhibit superior performance during restrictive monetary conditions. The return patterns of commodity futures are especially promising because the magnitude of the commodity futures return pattern is comparable to the stock return patterns but in the opposite direction (i.e., commodity futures exhibit returns that are four to five times higher during restrictive monetary conditions). Short-term T-bills also fare better during restrictive monetary periods. The performance differential, however, is relatively small. Although investors have traditionally been reluctant to invest in futures contracts, the development of futures markets, combined with the corresponding decrease in transaction costs, has increased the interest in this class of securities. Furthermore, in 1992, the Chicago Mercantile Exchange introduced a contract based on the Goldman Sachs Commodity Index (GSCI), which makes trading in a portfolio of commodity futures a relatively simple task.

Investment Implications

Throughout this monograph, we have generally presented the findings with relatively little discussion regarding the investment implications. The following discussion is presented in order to highlight the potential asset allocation benefits that could have been achieved by using monetary policy as a simple tactical allocation tool. Specifically, we present an example of the improvement in performance that a diversified U.S.-based investor could have achieved by using monetary conditions to allocate portfolio weights among five prominent security classes, and we compare an asset allocation strategy predicated on changes in monetary conditions with a buy-and-hold strategy. The following allocation strategy represents only one of many possible hypothetical situations and is presented as a rough illustration of possible strategies.

In order to prevent dramatic changes in the composition of the portfolio, we establish bounds on security weights. We require the investor to maintain a limited exposure to all five securities throughout; we set a ceiling on the investment in each security class; and we restrict short sales. Furthermore, our hypothetical investor is assumed to have an equity focus. Given these constraints, the five security classes and their corresponding minimum and maximum weights are shown in **Table 15**. These weights are designed to maintain a prominent investment in equities throughout all portfolios, to avoid extreme shifts in weightings during different monetary periods, and to limit the investment in the EAFE Index and the GSCI.

For our hypothetical investor, we first calculate the mean–variance efficient set of portfolios without respect to monetary conditions. We generate the efficient portfolios based on a quadratic programming approach and assume no riskless lending or borrowing and no short selling of securities. To use a full set of return data for all five securities, the sample period runs from January 1973 through December 1998. Consistent with the previous analyses, months that contain a change in monetary period are omitted from the analysis. **Table 16** reports the mean return and standard deviation of the resulting set of seven portfolios that are mean–variance efficient, with the related weights in each of the five security classes.

The findings indicate that each of the five securities plays a prominent role in determining the efficient set. As expected, the percentage of the portfolio invested in equities increases and the percentage invested in T-bills falls as the portfolio standard deviation increases. A notable observation is the prominent percentage that commodity futures (GSCI) and international securities (EAFE) constitute of the spectrum of efficient portfolios. This finding supports the contention of prior research that these security classes represent attractive investment vehicles (see Chance 1994 and Gorman 1998 for discussions of the related research). Although futures and international

Table 15. Portfolio Weights for Five Asset Classes

Security Class	Minimum Weight	Maximum Weight
U.S. stocks	30%	70%
International stocks (EAFE)	5	30
Corporate bonds	5	30
30-day T-bills	5	30
Commodity futures (GSCI)	5	30

Table 16. Efficient Portfolios: Buy-and-Hold Asset Weights

Portfolio	Mean Return	Standard Deviation	Security Weights				
			GSCI	U.S. Stock	30-Day T-Bill	Corporate Bond	EAFE
1	10.651%	6.582%	11.01%	30.00%	30.00%	23.90%	5.00%
2	10.994	6.928	16.10	30.00	24.50	21.90	7.50
3	11.430	7.621	18.40	30.00	13.60	27.80	10.20
4	11.855	8.314	20.80	30.00	5.00	29.90	14.40
5	12.228	9.007	21.80	35.60	5.00	21.80	15.90
6	12.562	9.699	22.60	40.90	5.00	14.40	17.10
7	12.883	10.392	23.40	46.10	5.00	7.40	18.20

equities are frequently considered relatively high-risk, stand-alone investments, they represent prominent percentages of both the *low-* and high-risk efficient portfolios. Many investors have recently accepted the benefits of investing in international equities, but the substantial weighting attributed to commodity futures is especially interesting because futures are not generally considered a viable alternative for the average investor.

Next, we allow the security weights to change in restrictive versus expansive monetary periods and determine which sets are mean–variance efficient. **Table 17** reports the risk and return profile of each portfolio (at the same standard deviation levels as in Table 16) and the security weights for periods of expansive and restrictive monetary policy. When compared with the mean returns in Table 16, the results in Table 17 indicate that tactical asset allocation based on monetary conditions can substantially improve portfolio performance. Because of the substantial adjustments to the weights, the higher the portfolio's risk, the more substantial the change in return. In contrast, the lower-risk portfolios were dominated by fixed-income securities in both monetary periods, which limited the potential improvement in performance. For the highest-risk portfolio, the asset allocation strategy resulted in approximately a 3.8 percent (16.71 percent minus 12.88 percent from Table 16) annual improvement in returns without any change in risk. Although transaction costs would have reduced this advantage somewhat, transaction costs would have been low because only 11 changes in the monetary environment (a change from a restrictive to an expansive Fed monetary policy or vice versa) occurred during the entire period.

Table 17. Efficient Portfolios Rebalanced According to Monetary Conditions

Security Weights in Expansive (Exp) and Restrictive (Res) Periods

Portfolio	Mean Return	Standard Deviation	GSCI		U.S. Stock		30-Day T-Bill		Corporate Bond		EAFE	
			Exp	Res	Exp	Res	Exp	Res	Exp	Res	Exp	Res
1	11.09%	6.58%	5.0%	8.6%	30.0%	30.0%	30.0%	30.0%	26.1%	26.4%	8.9%	5.0%
2	11.67	6.93	5.0	8.6	30.0	30.0	22.0	30.0	29.4	26.4	13.6	5.0
3	13.26	7.62	5.0	20.3	30.0	30.0	15.8	30.0	30.0	14.7	19.2	5.0
4	14.35	8.31	5.0	26.8	32.7	30.0	10.5	30.0	30.0	8.2	21.8	5.0
5	15.17	9.01	5.0	30.0	36.0	30.0	5.1	30.0	30.0	5.0	23.9	5.0
6	16.09	9.70	5.0	30.0	46.2	30.0	5.0	30.0	14.8	5.0	28.9	5.0
7	16.71	10.39	5.0	30.0	55.0	30.0	5.0	30.0	5.0	5.0	30.0	5.0

The allocation weights in the two alternative monetary periods provide several interesting results. First, in expansive monetary periods, commodity futures make unattractive investments. If not for the 5 percent minimum investment floor set for commodity futures, the optimal allocation to futures during expansive periods would be 0 percent. On the other hand, during restrictive periods, futures make very attractive investments and the allocation to this asset class is quite large. In fact, if not for the ceiling of 30 percent set on futures, the higher-risk portfolios would consist largely of commodity futures during restrictive monetary periods. Second, the equity securities, both U.S. and international, dominate the higher-risk portfolios during expansive periods. If not for their established floors, however, these securities would have a miniscule weighting during restrictive periods. In fact, during restrictive periods, the minimum weighting is applied for both U.S. and international stocks for all of the portfolios. Third, during restrictive periods, T-bills constitute a large percentage in all portfolios, even the highest-risk portfolios. For restrictive monetary conditions, the maximum weight is allocated to T-bills in all of the portfolios.

Note that the hypothetical portfolio may understate the benefits of using monetary policy to allocate assets. This understatement occurs for several reasons. First, the analysis focused on general asset classes and ignored subcategories of securities. Without question, asset allocation would have improved returns more dramatically had the allocation considered subcategories, such as industry affiliation for equities, emerging market equities, and alternative market-cap stocks (as discussed in Chapter 4). Second, we limited the adjustment in weights to avoid extreme changes in the composition of the portfolio and to prevent some securities from having zero weights. Third, the hypothetical situation is designed for a diversified investor with an emphasis on equities. The evidence reported in Table 3 of Chapter 3, however, indicates that a fixed-income investor historically could have improved performance by adjusting the bond portfolio maturity. Specifically, expansive monetary periods have favored longer maturity instruments, and restrictive periods have favored shorter maturity securities (particularly the 90-day T-bills). Thus, a fixed-income investor could have improved portfolio performance by lengthening the portfolio's maturity during expansive periods and reducing it during restrictive periods.

Conclusion

The evidence presented throughout this analysis is necessarily derived by examining historical returns. Thus, its relevance for future security returns should be interpreted with some caution. The general applicability and robustness of the results, however, are supported by several observations. First, the return patterns are found to be both statistically and economically significant. Further, the patterns persist over time, rather than resulting from a few extreme observations. Second, the return patterns are documented relative to Federal Reserve monetary policy, an economic variable that is widely acknowledged as a key factor in financial markets. Third, the return patterns are shown to exist for a variety of asset classes, which suggests that, for the securities markets as a whole, a fundamental difference exists between restrictive and expansive monetary periods. Finally, the return patterns do not vary with different measures of monetary policy. Although this study relies on Federal Reserve discount rate changes to identify monetary periods, the analysis in Chapter 5 indicates that other measures of monetary conditions are also related to the security return patterns.

Historically, as described in this chapter, a relatively simple allocation strategy designed to account for return patterns related to monetary policy would have provided a substantial enhancement in portfolio performance. The fact that the strategy relies on a variable that is both widely disseminated and recognized to have economic value raises the question of why the opportunity was not exploited by investors and ultimately eliminated through arbitrage. Several explanations are possible. First, much of the benefit achieved from the strategy accrues from the attractive performance exhibited by commodity futures during restrictive monetary periods. Although commodity futures are becoming more recognized as an acceptable investment vehicle, many investment managers still consider these investments to be inappropriate. In addition, managers are forced to operate within institutional constraints, which frequently prohibit, or at least severely restrict, the proportion of their portfolios that can be allocated to futures contracts. Also, our results are based on taking a diversified position in futures contracts. Recent innovations, such as the GSCI contract traded on the Chicago Mercantile Exchange and the Oppenheimer Real Asset Fund, have made such positions more practical. These investment vehicles, however, were not available for much of the study period.

A second possibility is that many investment managers have little discretion over the asset classes in which they invest because of style benchmarking. Fund managers are generally prohibited from deviating substantially from a fund's stated investment objective. For example, discretionary equity fund managers generally have the latitude to shift assets among various subcategories of equities, but they are prevented from reallocating a substantial proportion of the portfolio into money market instruments or commodity futures.

A third reason is that investment managers are evaluated relative to their peers on a fairly short-term basis. In contrast, our results reflect the average performance over a lengthy time period. In other words, the proposed strategy, although attractive in the long run, does not provide superior returns every period. Thus, fund managers may be reluctant to engage in substantial asset reallocations, even if they believe that, on average, the move is warranted. If the stock and bond markets perform poorly, investors can more readily accept poor performance from a fund manager. In contrast, the manager of a fund that performs poorly when the markets are prospering is likely to be replaced.

Finally, although the ideas expressed in our research are consistent with many investors' general investment philosophies, this research represents the first publication of a rigorous statistical analysis of a formal investment strategy based on the philosophy. Hence, prior to this research, the number of investment professionals who were aware of the magnitude of the potential benefits from the strategy was probably limited.

Appendix A. Industry Definitions

Industry	SIC Code
Mining	10–14
Food	20
Apparel	22–23
Paper	26
Chemical	28
Petroleum	29
Construction	32
Primary metals	33
Fabricated metals	34
Machinery	35
Electrical equipment	36
Transportation equipment	37
Manufacturing	38–39
Railroads	40
Other transportation	41–47
Utilities	49
Retail	50–52, 54–59
Department stores	53
Financial	60–69

Appendix B. Construction of the Goldman Sachs Commodity Index (GSCI)

Consistent with Strongin and Petsch (1999), which is the source for the following information, "GSCI" is used throughout this monograph to describe the total return index. The GSCI is world-production weighted, and the quantity of each commodity is determined by the average production of the commodity over the previous five years. The index includes all commodities offering sufficient liquidity and futures contract investability. Currently, the GSCI consists of 22 commodities from three broad categories distributed as follows: four energy products, nine metals, and nine agricultural products. The GSCI returns are calculated based on the arithmetic average of returns to long positions in futures contracts that are nearest to expiration. At the beginning of the expiration month, futures contracts that are near to expiration are exchanged for contracts with the next applicable expiration date. Actively traded contracts (e.g., energy and industrial metals) have contracts that expire monthly and are thus rolled forward on a monthly basis. Less actively traded contracts (e.g., agricultural and livestock) are rolled forward on a less frequent basis. The expiring contracts are rolled into the new contracts over a five-day roll period that occurs on the fifth through the ninth business days of the month. The rolls occur at a rate of 20 percent a day and are assumed to occur at the daily settlement price at the end of each of the five rolling-period days. The final GSCI return is calculated by adding the T-bill return to the return obtained from the long position in the futures contracts. This return represents a fully collateralized return and is thus comparable to the returns earned from long positions in equities and bonds.

References

Ankrim, Ernest, and Chris Hensel. 1993. "Commodities in Asset Allocation: A Real Alternative to Real Estate?" *Financial Analysts Journal*, vol. 49, no. 3 (May/June):20–29.

Banz, Rolf. 1981. "The Relationship between Return and Market Value of Common Stocks." *Journal of Financial Economics*, vol. 9, no. 1 (March):3–18.

Basu, Sanjoy. 1983. "The Relationship between Earnings' Yield, Market Value and Return for NYSE Common Stocks: Further Evidence." *Journal of Financial Economics*, vol. 12, no. 1 (June):129–156.

Bernanke, Ben S. 1990. "On the Predictive Power of Interest Rates and Interest Rate Spreads." *New England Economic Review* (November/December):51–68.

Bernanke, Ben S., and Alan S. Blinder. 1992. "The Federal Funds Rate and the Channels of Monetary Transmission." *American Economic Review*, vol. 82, no. 4 (September):901–921.

Bernard, V.L., and T.J. Frecka. 1983. "Evidence on the Existence of Common Stock Inflation Hedges." *Journal of Financial Research*, vol. 6, no. 4 (Winter):301–312.

Bjornson, Bruce, and Colin A. Carter. 1997. "New Evidence on Agricultural Commodity Return Performance under Time-Varying Risk." *American Journal of Agricultural Economics*, vol. 79, no. 3 (August):918–930.

Board of Governors of the Federal Reserve. 1961. *The Federal Reserve System: Purposes and Functions*. Washington, DC: Board of Governors.

Bodie, Zvi. 1983. "Commodity Futures as a Hedge Against Inflation." *Journal of Portfolio Management*, vol. 9, no. 3 (Spring):12–17.

Bodie, Zvi, and Victor Rosansky. 1980. "Risk and Return in Commodity Futures." *Financial Analysts Journal*, vol. 36, no. 3 (May/June):27–39.

Booth, James R., and Lena Chua Booth. 1997. "Economic Factors, Monetary Policy, and Expected Returns on Stocks and Bonds." *Economic Review: Federal Reserve Bank of San Francisco*:32–42.

Campbell, John. 1987. "Stock Returns and the Term Structure." *Journal of Financial Economics*, vol. 18, no. 2 (June):373–399.

Chan, K.C., and Nai-Fu Chen. 1991. "Structural and Return Characteristics of Small and Large Firms." *Journal of Finance*, vol. 46, no. 4 (September):1467–84.

Chance, Don. 1994. *Managed Futures and Their Role in Investment Portfolios*. Charlottesville, VA: Research Foundation of the Institute of Chartered Financial Analysts.

Cole, Kevin, Jean Helwege, and David Laster. 1996. "Stock Market Valuation Indicators: Is This Time Different?" *Financial Analysts Journal*, vol. 52, no. 3 (May/June):56–64.

Conover, C. Mitchell, Gerald Jensen, and Robert Johnson. 1999a. "Monetary Conditions and International Investing." *Financial Analysts Journal*, vol. 55, no. 4 (July/August):38–48.

———. 1999b. "Monetary Environments and International Stock Returns." *Journal of Banking and Finance*, vol. 23, no. 9 (September):1357–81.

Cook, Timothy, and Thomas Hahn. 1988. "The Information Content of Discount Rate Announcements and Their Effect on Market Interest Rates." *Journal of Money, Credit and Banking*, vol. 20, no. 2 (May):167–180.

Edwards, Franklin R., and Jimmy Liew. 1999. "Managed Commodity Funds." *Journal of Futures Markets*, vol. 19, no. 4 (June):377–411.

Edwards, Franklin R., and James M. Park. 1996. "Do Managed Futures Make Good Investments?" *Journal of Futures Markets*, vol. 16, no. 5 (August):475–517.

Elton, Edwin, Martin Gruber, and Joel Rentzler. 1987. "Professionally Managed, Publicly Traded Commodity Funds." *Journal of Business*, vol. 60, no. 2 (April):177–199.

Fama, Eugene F. 1990. "Stock Returns, Expected Returns, and Real Activity." *Journal of Finance*, vol. 45, no. 4 (September):1089–1108.

Fama, Eugene F., and Kenneth R. French. 1988. "Dividend Yields and Expected Stock Returns." *Journal of Financial Economics*, vol. 22, no. 1 (October):3–25.

———. 1989. "Business Conditions and Expected Returns on Stocks and Bonds." *Journal of Financial Economics*, vol. 25, no. 1 (November):23–49.

———. 1992. "The Cross-Section of Expected Stock Returns." *Journal of Finance*, vol. 47, no. 2 (June):427–465.

———. 1995. "Size and Book-to-Market Factors in Earnings and Returns." *Journal of Finance*, vol. 50, no. 1 (March):131–155.

Fama, Eugene F., and William Schwert. 1977. "Asset Returns and Inflation." *Journal of Financial Economics*, vol. 5, no. 2 (November):115–146.

Ferson, Wayne, and Campbell Harvey. 1999. "Conditioning Variables and the Cross-Section of Stock Returns." *Journal of Finance*, vol. 54, no. 4 (August):1325–60.

Friedman, Benjamin M., and Kenneth N. Kuttner. 1992. "Time-Varying Risk Perceptions and the Pricing of Risky Assets." *Oxford Economic Papers*, vol. 44, no. 4 (October):566–598.

Friedman, Milton. 1959. *A Program for Monetary Stability*. New York: Fordham University Press.

Gertler, Mark, and Simon Gilchrist. 1994. "Monetary Policy, Business Cycles, and the Behavior of Small Manufacturing Firms." *Quarterly Journal of Economics*, vol. 109, no. 2 (May):309–340.

Goldman Sachs. 1996. *Goldman Sachs Commodities Index Manual*. New York: Goldman, Sachs & Company.

Gorman, Stephen A. 1998. *The International Equity Commitment*. Charlottesville, VA: Research Foundation of the Institute of Chartered Financial Analysts.

Grubel, Herbert G. 1968. "Internationally Diversified Portfolios: Welfare Gains and Capital Flows." *American Economic Review*, vol. 58, no. 5 (December):1299–1314.

Harris, Robert, and Felicia Marston. 1994. "Value Versus Growth Stocks: Book-to-Market, Growth, and Beta." *Financial Analysts Journal*, vol. 50, no. 5 (September/October):18–24.

Ho, Thomas S.Y., and Anthony Saunders. 1985. "A Micro Model of the Federal Funds Market." *Journal of Finance*, vol. 40, no. 3 (July): 977–988.

Irwin, Scott H., and B. Wade Brorsen. 1985. "Public Futures Funds." *The Journal of Futures Markets*, vol. 5, no. 2 (Summer):149–171.

Irwin, Scott H., and Diego Landa. 1987. "Real Estate, Futures, and Gold as Portfolio Assets." *Journal of Portfolio Management*, vol. 14, no. 1 (Fall):29–34.

Jacobs, Bruce I., and Kenneth N. Levy. 1989. "The Complexity of the Stock Market." *Journal of Portfolio Management*, vol. 16, no. 1 (Fall):19–27.

Jagannathan, Ravi, and Zhenyu Wang. 1996. "The Conditional CAPM and the Cross-Section of Expected Returns." *Journal of Finance*, vol. 51, no. 1 (March):3–53.

Jensen, Gerald R., and Robert R. Johnson. 1995. "Discount Rate Changes and Security Returns in the U.S., 1962–1991." *Journal of Banking and Finance*, vol. 19, no. 1 (April):79–95.

Jensen, Gerald R., Robert R. Johnson, and Jeffrey M. Mercer. 1997. "New Evidence on Size and Price-to-Book Effects in Stock Returns." *Financial Analysts Journal*, vol. 53, no. 6 (November/December):34–42.

———. 1998. "The Inconsistency of Small-Firm and Value Stock Premiums." *Journal of Portfolio Management*, vol. 24, no. 2 (Winter):27–36.

———. 2000. "Efficient Use of Commodity Futures in Diversified Portfolios." *Journal of Futures Markets*, vol. 20, no. 5 (May):489–506.

Jensen, Gerald R., Jeffrey M. Mercer, and Robert R. Johnson. 1996. "Business Conditions, Monetary Policy, and Expected Security Returns." *Journal of Financial Economics*, vol. 40, no. 2 (February):213–237.

Jones, David M. 1989. *Fed Watching and Interest Rate Projections*. New York: New York Institute of Finance.

Keim, Donald. 1990. "A New Look at the Effect of Firm Size and E/P Ratio on Stock Returns." *Financial Analysts Journal*, vol. 46, no. 2 (March/April):56–67.

Keim, Donald, and Robert F. Stambaugh. 1986. "Predicting Returns in the Stock and Bond Markets." *Journal of Financial Economics*, vol. 17, no. 2 (December):357–390.

Kothari, S.P., Jay Shanken, and Richard Sloan. 1995. "Another Look at the Cross-Section of Expected Stock Returns." *Journal of Finance*, vol. 50, no. 1 (March):185–224.

Laurent, Robert. 1988. "An Interest Rate-Based Indicator of Monetary Policy." *Economic Perspectives* (January/February):3–14.

Lee, Cheng, Raymond Leuthold, and Jean Cordier. 1985. "The Stock Market and Commodities Futures Market: Diversification and Arbitrage Potential." *Financial Analysts Journal*, vol. 41, no. 4 (July/August):53–60.

Lessard, Donald. 1976. "World, Country, and Industry Relationships in Equity Returns." *Financial Analysts Journal*, vol. 32, no. 1 (January/February):32–38.

Levy, Haim, and Marshall Sarnat. 1970. "Alternative Efficiency Criteria: An Empirical Analysis." *Journal of Finance*, vol. 25, no. 5 (December):1153–58.

Ma, Christopher K., and M.E. Ellis. 1989. "Selecting Industries as Inflation Hedges." *Journal of Portfolio Management*, vol. 15, no. 4 (Summer):45–48.

McNess, Stephen K. 1993. "The Discount Rate: The Other Tool of Monetary Policy." *New England Economic Review* (July/August):3–22.

Moskowitz, Tobias, and Mark Grinblatt. 1999. "Do Industries Explain Momentum?" *Journal of Finance*, vol. 54, no. 4 (August):1249–90.

Nowak, Laura S. 1993. *Monetary Policy and Investment Opportunities*. Westport, CT: Quorum Books.

Ogden, Joseph. 1987. "The End of the Month as a Preferred Habitat: A Test of Operational Efficiency in the Money Market." *Journal of Financial and Quantitative Analysis*, vol. 22, no. 3 (September):329–343.

———. 1990. "Turn-of-Month Evaluations of Liquid Profits and Stock Returns: A Common Explanation for the Monthly and January Effects." *Journal of Finance*, vol. 45, no. 4 (September):1259–72

Patelis, Alex. 1997. "Stock Return Predictability and the Role of the Monetary Sector." *Journal of Finance*, vol. 52, no. 5 (June):1951–72.

Pearce, Douglas, and V. Vance Roley. 1985. "Stock Prices and Economic News." *Journal of Business*, vol. 58, no. 1 (January):49–67.

Prather, Laurie, and William Bertin. 1997. "A Simple and Effective Trading Rule for Individual Investors." *Financial Services Review* (Index Issue):285–294.

Reinganum, Marc. 1981. "Misspecification of Capital Asset Pricing: Empirical Anomalies Based on Earnings' Yields and Market Values." *Journal of Financial Economics*, vol. 9, no. 1 (March):19–46.

———. 1988. "The Anatomy of a Stock Market Winner." *Financial Analysts Journal*, vol. 44, no. 2 (March/April):16–28.

Romer, Christina, and David Romer. 1996. "Federal Reserve Private Information and the Behavior of Interest Rates." NBER Working Paper 5692.

Rosenberg, Barr, Kenneth Reid, and Ronald Lanstein. 1985. "Persuasive Evidence of Market Inefficiency." *Journal of Portfolio Management*, vol. 11, no. 3 (Spring):9–16.

Schwert, G. Williams. 1990. "Stock Returns and Real Activity: A Century of Evidence." *Journal of Finance*, vol. 45, no. 4 (October):1237–57.

Sinquefield, Rex. 1996. "Where Are the Gains from International Diversification?" *Financial Analysts Journal*, vol. 52, no. 1 (January/February):8–14.

Smirlock, Michael J., and Jess B. Yawitz. 1985. "Asset Returns, Discount Rate Changes, and Market Efficiency." *Journal of Finance*, vol. 40, no. 4 (September):1141–58.

Solnik, B.H. 1974. "The International Pricing of Risk: An Empirical Investigation of the World Capital Market Structure." *Journal of Finance*, vol. 29, no. 2 (May):365–378.

Stock, James, and Mark Watson. 1989. "Interpreting the Evidence on Money-Income Causality." *Journal of Econometrics*, vol. 40, no. 1 (January):161–181.

Strongin, Steve, and Melanie Petsch. 1999. "Goldman Sachs Commodity Index (GSCI)." Published by Goldman, Sachs & Company on the Web: www.gs.com/gsci.

Thorbecke, Willem. 1997. "On Stock Market Returns and Monetary Policy." *Journal of Finance*, vol. 52, no. 2 (June):635–654.

Thornton, Daniel. 1998. "The Information Content of Discount Rate Announcements: What Is Behind the Announcement Effect?" *Journal of Banking and Finance*, vol. 22, no. 1 (January):83–108.

Waud, Roger N. 1970. "Public Interpretation of Federal Reserve Discount Rate Changes: Evidence on the Announcement Effect." *Econometrica*, vol. 38, no. 2 (March):231–250.

Yamada, Louise. 1998. *Market Magic: Riding the Greatest Bull Market of the Century.* New York: John Wiley & Sons, Inc.

Zweig, Martin E. 1986. *Martin Zweig's Winning on Wall Street.* New York: Warner Books.

Selected AIMR Publications

AIMR Performance Presentation Standards Handbook, 2nd edition, 1997

Alternative Investing, 1998

Asian Equity Investing, 1998

Asset Allocation in a Changing World, 1998

Credit Analysis Around the World, 1998

Currency Risk in Investment Portfolios, 1999

Derivatives in Portfolio Management, 1998

Ethical Issues for Today's Firm, 2000

Equity Research and Valuation Techniques, 1998

Frontiers in Credit-Risk Analysis, 1999

The Future of Investment Management, 1998

Global Bond Management II: The Search for Alpha, 2000

Investment Counseling for Private Clients, 1999

Investment Counseling for Private Clients II, 2000

Practical Issues in Equity Analysis, 2000

Risk Management: Principles and Practices, 1999

Standards of Practice Handbook, 8th edition, 1999

The Technology Industry: Impact of the Internet, 2000

A full catalog of publications is available on AIMR's World Wide Web site at **www.aimr.org**; or you may write to AIMR, P.O. Box 3668, Charlottesville, VA 22903 U.S.A.; call 1-804-951-5499; fax 1-804-951-5262; or e-mail **info@aimr.org** to receive a free copy. All prices are subject to change.

BLACKWELL Publishers

9 780943 205502

90000